EYEWITNESS
KNIGHT

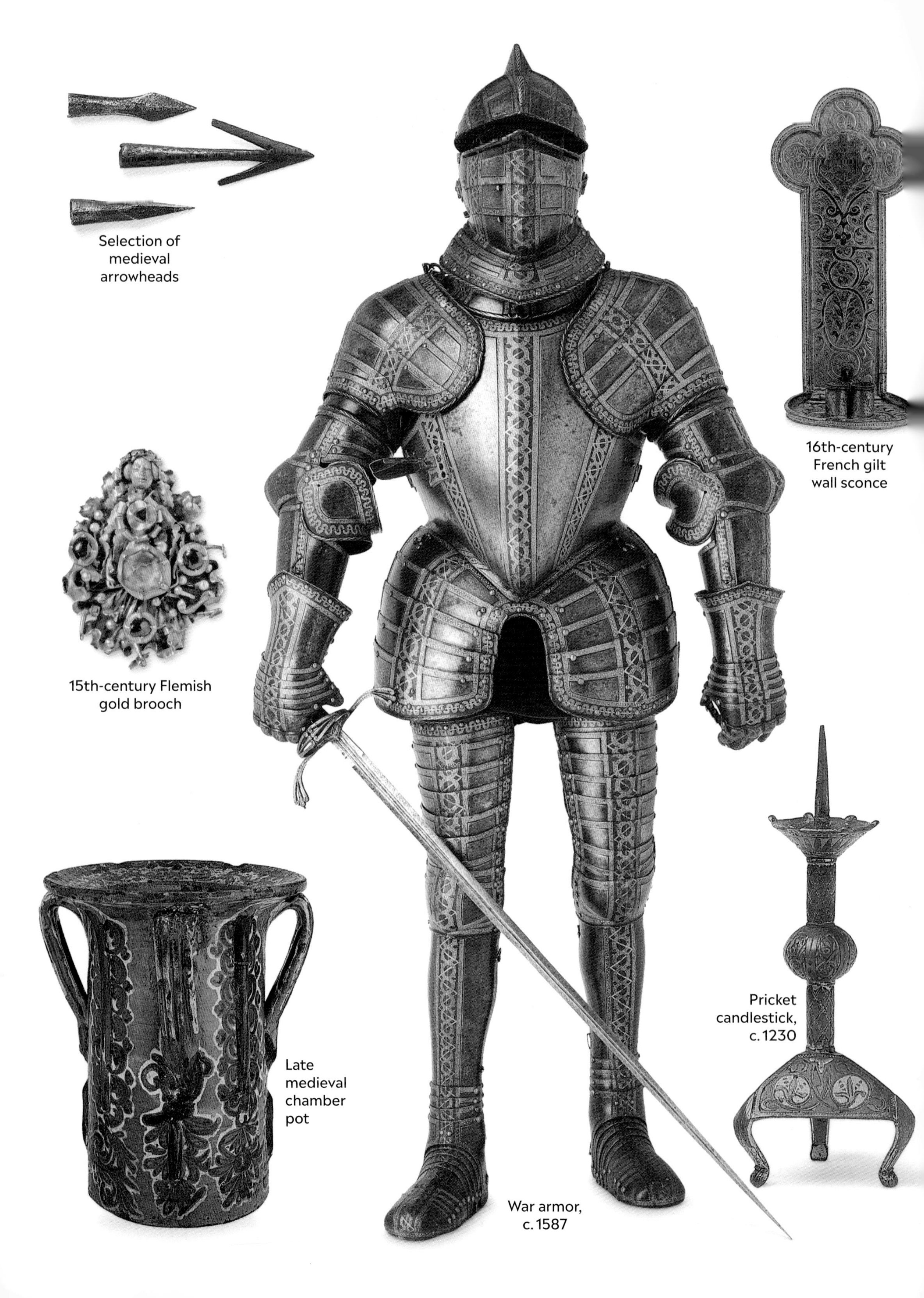

Selection of medieval arrowheads

16th-century French gilt wall sconce

15th-century Flemish gold brooch

Pricket candlestick, c. 1230

Late medieval chamber pot

War armor, c. 1587

KNIGHT

Written by
CHRISTOPHER GRAVETT

Photographed by
GEOFF DANN

16th-century Italian parade helmet

15th-century German serving knife

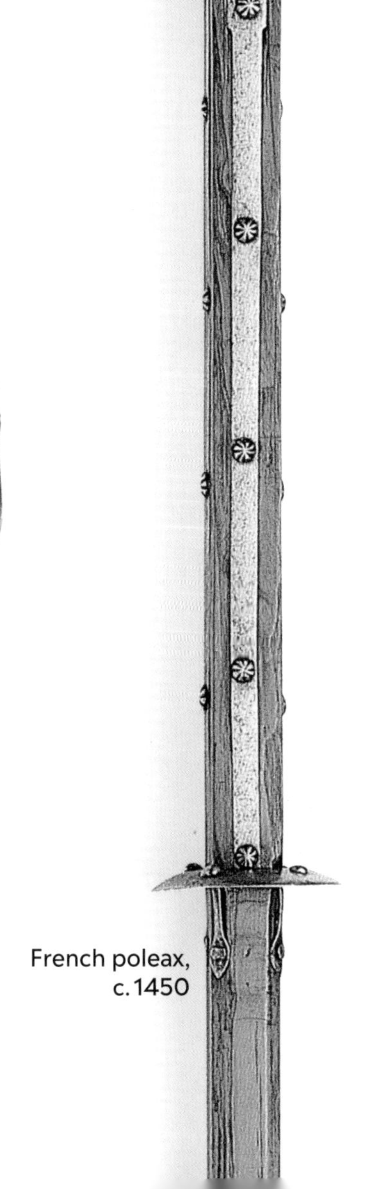

French poleax, c. 1450

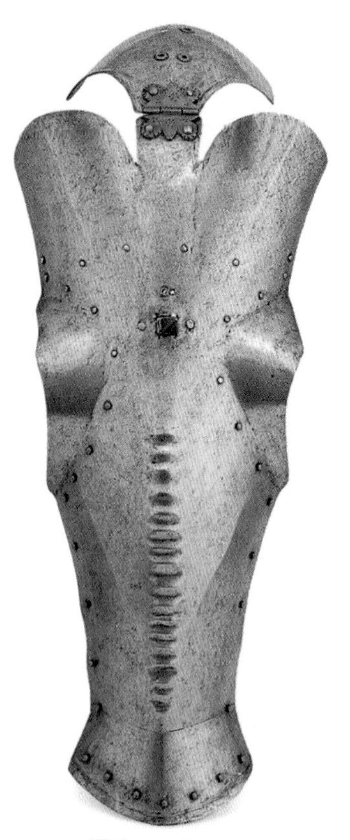

15th-century
Flemish chaffron

15th-century spur

German
halberd,
c. 1500

REVISED EDITION

DK DELHI
Senior Art Editor Vikas Chauhan
Art Editors Tanvi Sahu, Astha Singh
Assistant Editor Vandana Likhmania
Assistant Art Editor Prateek Maurya
Team Lead, Picture Research Sumedha Chopra
Deputy Manager, Picture Research Virien Chopra
Deputy Managing Editor Sreshtha Bhattacharya
Managing Editor Kingshuk Ghoshal
Managing Art Editor Govind Mittal
DTP Designers Nand Kishor Acharya, Rakesh Kumar
Production Editor Pawan Kumar
Project Jacket Designer Juhi Sheth
Senior Jackets Coordinator Priyanka Sharma Saddi
DK India Creative Head Malavika Talukder

DK LONDON
Senior Editor Rona Skene **Art Editor** Beth Johnston
Senior US Editor Megan Douglass
US Executive Editor Lori Cates Hand
Managing Editor Francesca Baines
Managing Art Editor Philip Letsu
Production Controller Jack Matts
Jacket Design Development Manager Sophia MTT
Publisher Andrew Macintyre
Art Director Mabel Chan
Managing Director Sarah Larter

Consultant Christopher Gravett

FIRST EDITION
Project Editor Phil Wilkinson
Art Editor Ann Cannings
Managing Editor Helen Parker
Managing Art Editor Julia Harris
Production Louise Barratt
Picture Research Kathy Lockley

This American Edition, 2024
First American Edition, 1993
Published in the United States by DK Publishing,
a division of Penguin Random House LLC
1745 Broadway, 20th Floor, New York, NY 10019

24 25 26 27 28 10 9 8 7 6 5 4 3 2 1
001-341830-Dec/2024

Published in Great Britain by Dorling Kindersley Limited

A catalog record for this book is available
from the Library of Congress.
ISBN 978-0-5938-4383-3 (Paperback)
ISBN 978-0-5938-4384-0 (ALB)

Printed and bound in China

www.dk.com

Plaque showing a knight
on horseback

Italian
sword,
c. 1460

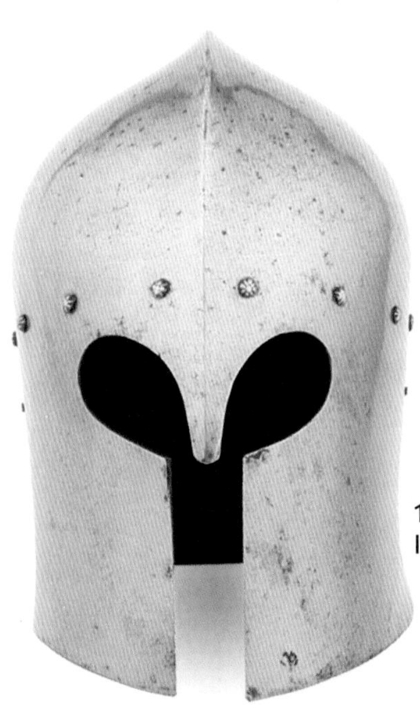

15th-century
Italian barbute

Contents

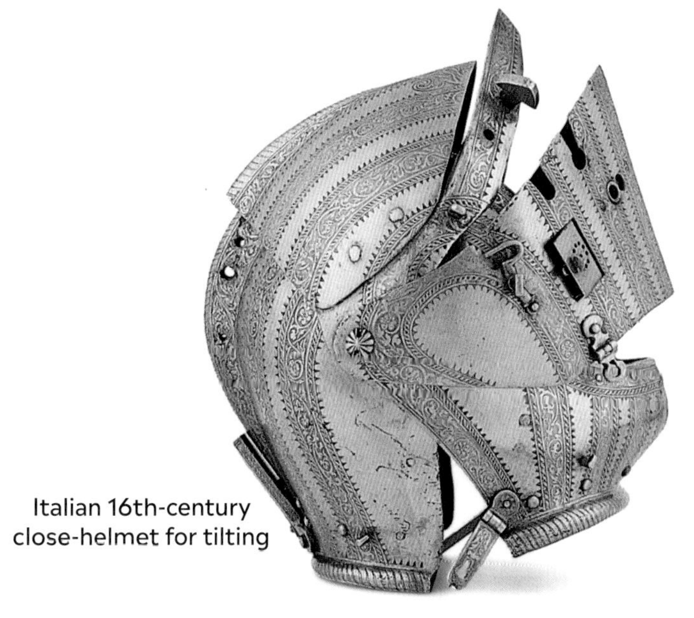

Italian 16th-century close-helmet for tilting

6
The first knights

8
The Normans

10
Making a knight

12
Armor

14
Fashion in steel

16
Inside the armor

18
Arms and the man

20
On horseback

22
The castle

24
The castle at war

26
Siege warfare

28
Armed to fight

30
The enemy

32
Into battle

34
Castle life

36
Manor lords

38
Manor ladies

40
The ideal of chivalry

42
The tournament

44
The joust

46
Foot combat

48
Heraldry

50
Hunting

52
Faith and pilgrimage

54
The crusades

56
Knights of Christ

58
Japanese knights

60
The professionals

62
Knights' end

64
Did you know?

66
Timeline

68
Find out more

70
Glossary

72
Index

The first **knights**

In the fifth century CE barbarian tribes invaded the collapsing Roman Empire and Europe. A group called the Franks expanded their power, and in 800 CE their leader, Charlemagne, became Emperor of the West. In the ninth century, this empire broke up into smaller pieces. Powerful lords and their warriors offered protection to peasants who became serfs to the lords, which meant losing their freedom. During the 10th century these warriors, trained to fight from horseback, became known as knights. A new social order, called feudalism, was gradually formed in which armored knights served a local lord, count, or duke.

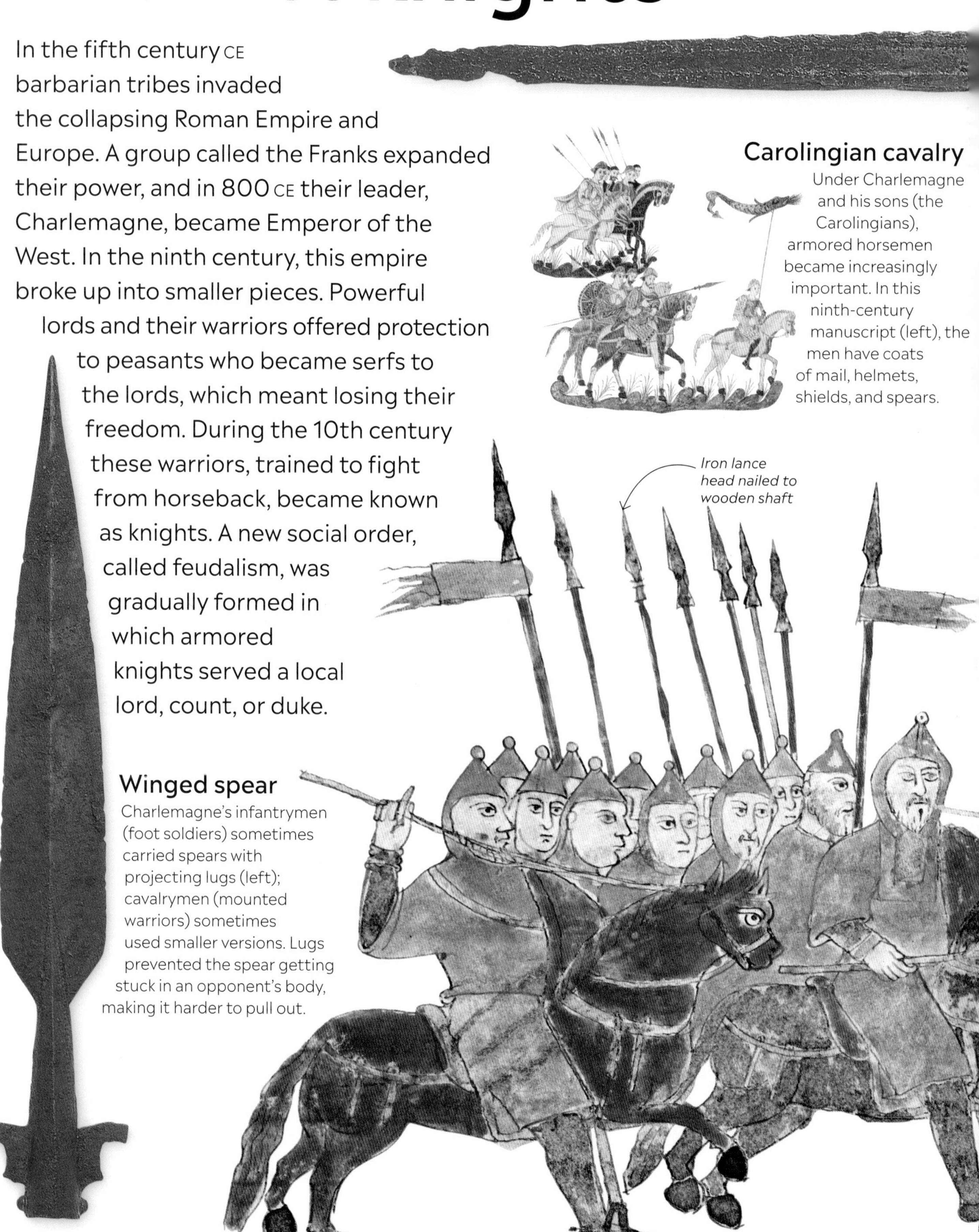

Carolingian cavalry

Under Charlemagne and his sons (the Carolingians), armored horsemen became increasingly important. In this ninth-century manuscript (left), the men have coats of mail, helmets, shields, and spears.

Winged spear

Charlemagne's infantrymen (foot soldiers) sometimes carried spears with projecting lugs (left); cavalrymen (mounted warriors) sometimes used smaller versions. Lugs prevented the spear getting stuck in an opponent's body, making it harder to pull out.

utting edge

he double-edged slashing sword was the most highly rized of weapons and the most difficult and expensive o make. At first only wealthy people could afford one, so he sword became the typical weapon of the knight.

Kings and nobles

The king and all his nobles were knights. This 10th-century scene shows the king talking with his nobles.

Ax-head

he ax was popular among many uropean tribes who fought on foot. owever, it lost favor with the mounted knights. This ax-head is rom Germany, where feudalism and knighthood were slow in coming.

Stirrup

This 10th-century Lombard stirrup from Italy helped keep a warrior firm in his saddle. Stirrups appeared in western Europe in the early eighth century.

Charge!

In this Italian manuscript from 1028, knights wear mail coats (pp.12–13) with mail hoods and iron helmets. Straps around the horses' chests and hindquarters helped hold their saddles in place.

EYEWITNESS

Charlemagne
Charles I, also known as Charlemagne (c. 747–814), was a successful warrior king who ruled over much of western and central Europe. He also revived culture and learning. In 800, the pope crowned him "Emperor of the Romans."

The **Normans**

In an attempt to stop the Vikings raiding his territory, Charles III of France gave some land to a group of these "northmen" in 911. Their new home was called Normandy, and their leader, Rollo, became its first duke. The Vikings fought on foot, but the Normans, as they became known, adopted the French use of mounted knights. Duke William of Normandy brought his knights to England in 1066 and, after winning the Battle of Hastings, he built castles and introduced the feudal system.

Metal boss

Shielded from danger

This small 12th-century bronze figurine shows how knightly equipment slowly changed after the Norman conquest of England. The top of the helmet is tilted slightly forward, and the shield has a reinforcing metal boss in the center.

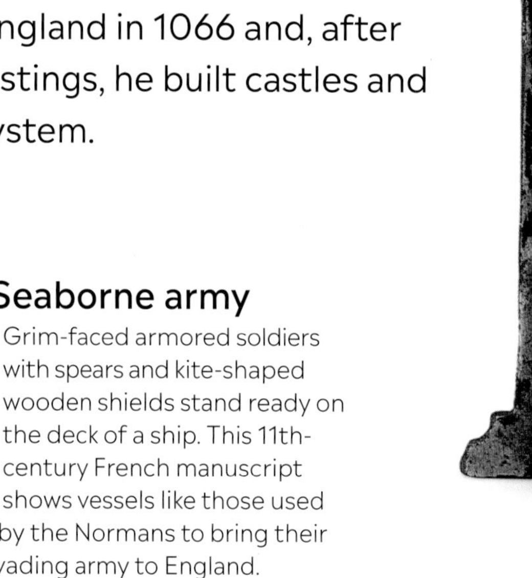

Seaborne army

Grim-faced armored soldiers with spears and kite-shaped wooden shields stand ready on the deck of a ship. This 11th-century French manuscript shows vessels like those used by the Normans to bring their invading army to England.

Shield wall

In this scene from the Bayeux Tapestry, an embroidery made within 20 years of the Battle of Hastings, the English (right) defend their hilltop position near Hastings. Unlike the Normans (left), the English fought wholly on foot. The armor of their higher-ranking troops is similar to that of the Normans. The English saw the Normans following their lord and called them "cnihtas" (youths, servants), from which comes the word "knights."

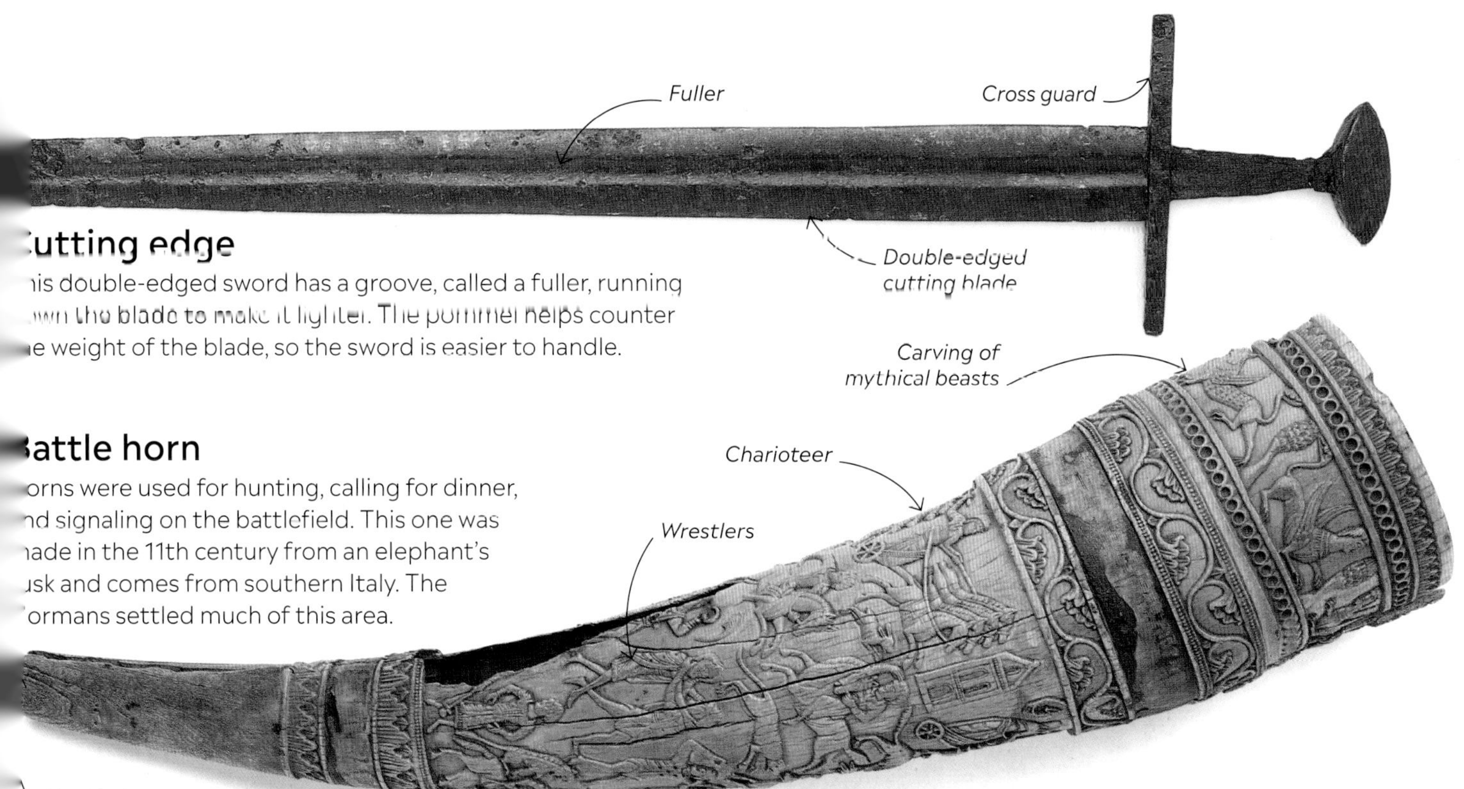

Cutting edge

This double-edged sword has a groove, called a fuller, running down the blade to make it lighter. The pommel helps counter the weight of the blade, so the sword is easier to handle.

Battle horn

Horns were used for hunting, calling for dinner, and signaling on the battlefield. This one was made in the 11th century from an elephant's tusk and comes from southern Italy. The Normans settled much of this area.

Solid faith

The Normans used stone to build some of their castles (pp.22–23), cathedrals, abbeys, and churches throughout England. They used the Romanesque style of architecture, which included large columns and rounded arches, seen here in the nave of Durham Cathedral.

EYEWITNESS

Odo of Bayeux
Half-brother of William of Normandy, Odo (c.1036–1097) was bishop of Bayeux. He fought at Hastings in 1066 and was made Earl of Kent. Odo probably commissioned the famous Bayeux Tapestry and appears in it multiple times. In this detail he is sitting on the left.

Making a **knight**

A boy of noble birth who hoped to become a knight was usually sent away at age seven to a nobleman's household to be a page. Here he learned how to behave and to ride a horse. When about 14, he was apprenticed to a knight, whom he served as a squire, and was taught to handle weapons, and even went into battle with the knight. Successful squires were knighted when they were around 21 years old.

Boy's cuirass

These pieces of armor from around 1600 are specially made to fit a boy. Only rich families could afford to give their young sons such a gift.

The page

A page learned a variety of skills, from serving a knight to the art of courtly manners and good breeding.

Practice makes perfect

Squires trained constantly to strengthen their muscles and improve their skill with weapons. Such training was hard and not everyone could manage it. Those who did, eventually went on to become knights. This 15th-century picture shows squires training in various disciplines.

Jousting practice

After striking the shield of a wooden, soldier-shaped structure (above), the rider had to pass by quickly to avoid the swinging weight.

The squire

In the 11th and 12th centuries, many squires were servants of a lower social class, while others were the sons of noble families training to become knights. In the 13th century, becoming a knight was so expensive that many men remained squires. By the 17th century, "squire" came to mean a landowning gentleman.

At the pel

Squires could practice against a wooden post, or pel. Sometimes they were given weapons double the weight to develop their muscles.

Wheel pommel for grip and balance

EYEWITNESS

Geoffrey Chaucer

English poet Geoffrey Chaucer (c. 1342–1400) gives us a vivid portrait of a squire in his most famous work *The Canterbury Tales.* He describes his squire as an athletic, cultured, romantic young man.

Thigh-length leather boots

Dubbing

A squire was finally made into a knight at the dubbing ceremony. This was originally a blow to the neck with the hand, but by the 13th century it was replaced by a tap with the sword. The knight's sword and spurs were fastened on and celebrations followed. Another knight, often the squire's master or the king, performed the dubbing.

Armor

Early knights wore armor made of small, linked iron rings called mail. During the 12th century knights started to wear more mail. By the 14th century, knights were adding steel plates to protect their limbs, and the body was protected further with a coat-of-plates made of pieces of iron riveted to a cloth covering. In the 15th century, knights wore full suits of plate armor. A suit weighed about 44–55 lb (20–25 kg), the weight being spread over the body so the knight could run, lie down, or mount a horse unaided.

Mail

Weighing about 20–31 lb (9–14 kg), most c the mail coat's weight was on the knight's shoulders. Each open ring is interlinked with four others and closed with a rivet.

Knightly plaque

This mounted knight from the 14th century has a helm fitted with a crest that identified him in battle. However, at this time, the basinet and visor were becoming popular.

Mail-maker

This 15th-century picture shows an armorer using pliers to join the links. He could shape the mail by increasing or reducing the number of links.

Basinet

This 14th-century Italian basinet was originally fitted with a visor that pivoted over the brow. But, at some point, a side-pivoting visor was fitted.

Pin allowing visor to be removed

Cord allowing mail to be removed

Ventilation holes

Later mail neck guard

Courtly gauntlets

Gauntlet plates, like this 14th-century pair from Milan, Italy, were riveted to a leather glove. Small plates were added to protect the fingers.

nhorsed

is 13th-century picture shows the large shields at protected knights from blows against flexible ail. By 1400, thanks to plate armor, shields had ecome much smaller.

EYEWITNESS

Tobias Capwell

US historian Dr. Tobias Capwell is an expert in medieval arms and armor, and is a former curator at the Wallace Collection, London. He participates in jousting tournaments in replica armor, and has written many books on the armor worn by English knights.

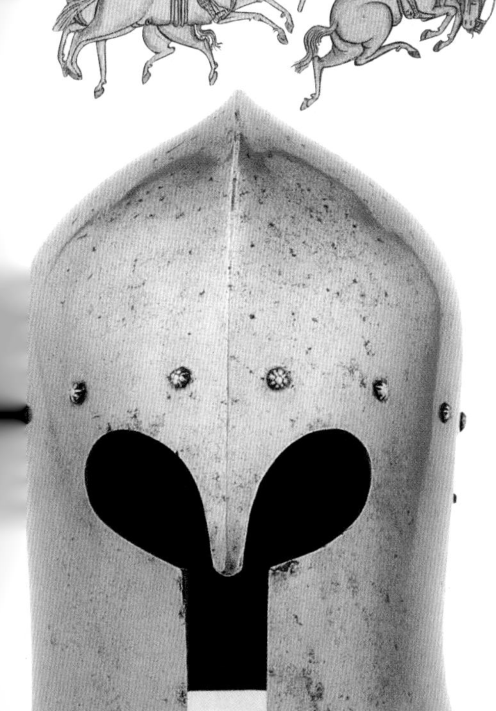

Barbute

Rivets around the helmets, like those on this Italian barbute from around 1470, held a padded lining inside. Rivets lower down originally held a leather chin strap to stop the helmet being knocked off.

Plate armor

The knight on the left, from c. 1340, wears mail and coat-of-plates, plus plate armor on his arms and legs. The knight on the right, from about 1420, has full plate armor.

Gauntlet

This German "Gothic" armor from the late 15th century gave better protection than mail because it was solid and did not flex when struck heavily by a weapon.

The mailed knight

This knight from around 1250 wears a cloth surcoat over his mail, perhaps in imitation of Muslim dress seen on crusade.

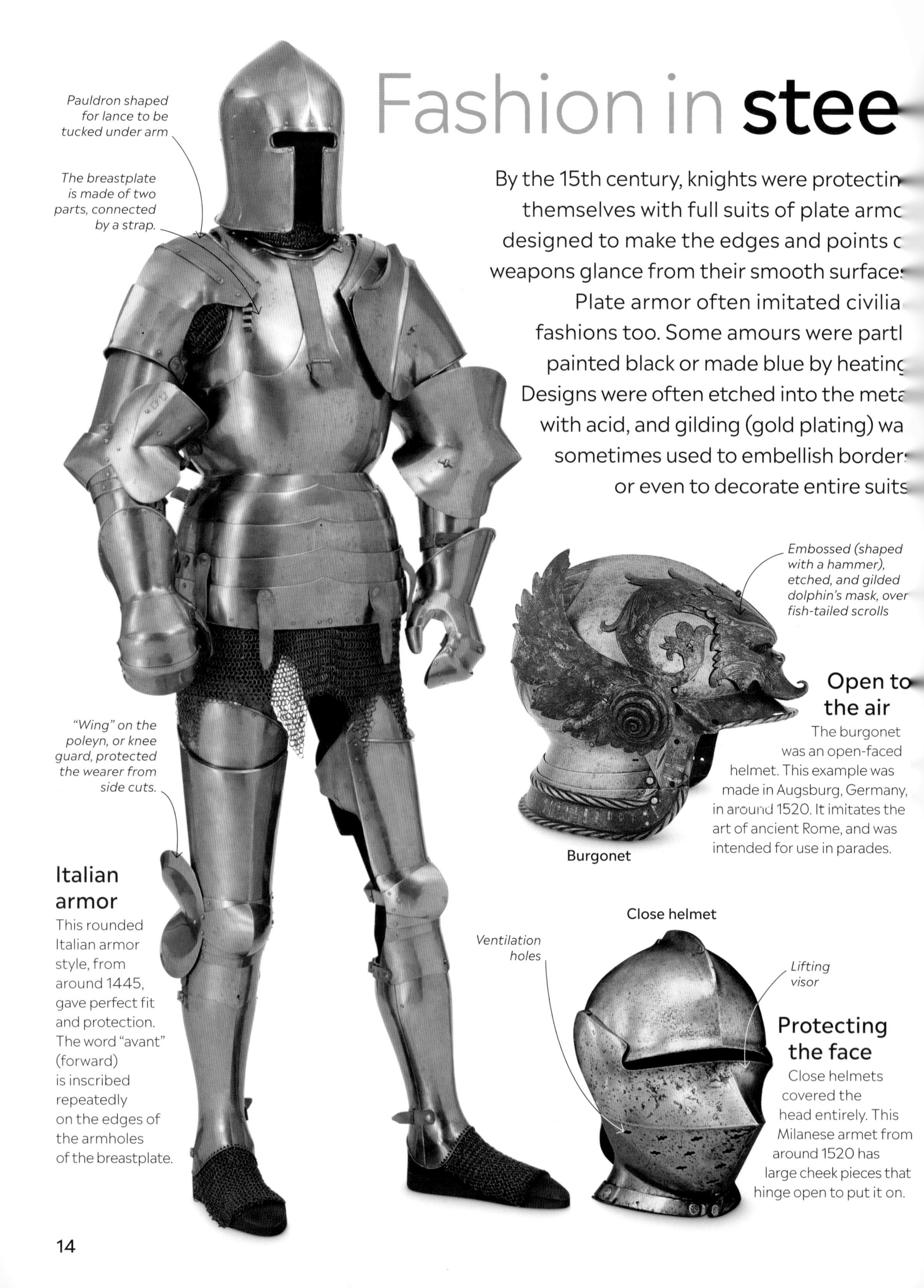

Fashion in stee

By the 15th century, knights were protectin themselves with full suits of plate armc designed to make the edges and points c weapons glance from their smooth surface: Plate armor often imitated civilia fashions too. Some amours were partl painted black or made blue by heatin Designs were often etched into the meta with acid, and gilding (gold plating) wa sometimes used to embellish border or even to decorate entire suits

Italian armor

This rounded Italian armor style, from around 1445, gave perfect fit and protection. The word "avant" (forward) is inscribed repeatedly on the edges of the armholes of the breastplate.

Burgonet

Open to the air

The burgonet was an open-faced helmet. This example was made in Augsburg, Germany, in around 1520. It imitates the art of ancient Rome, and was intended for use in parades.

Close helmet

Protecting the face

Close helmets covered the head entirely. This Milanese armet from around 1520 has large cheek pieces that hinge open to put it on.

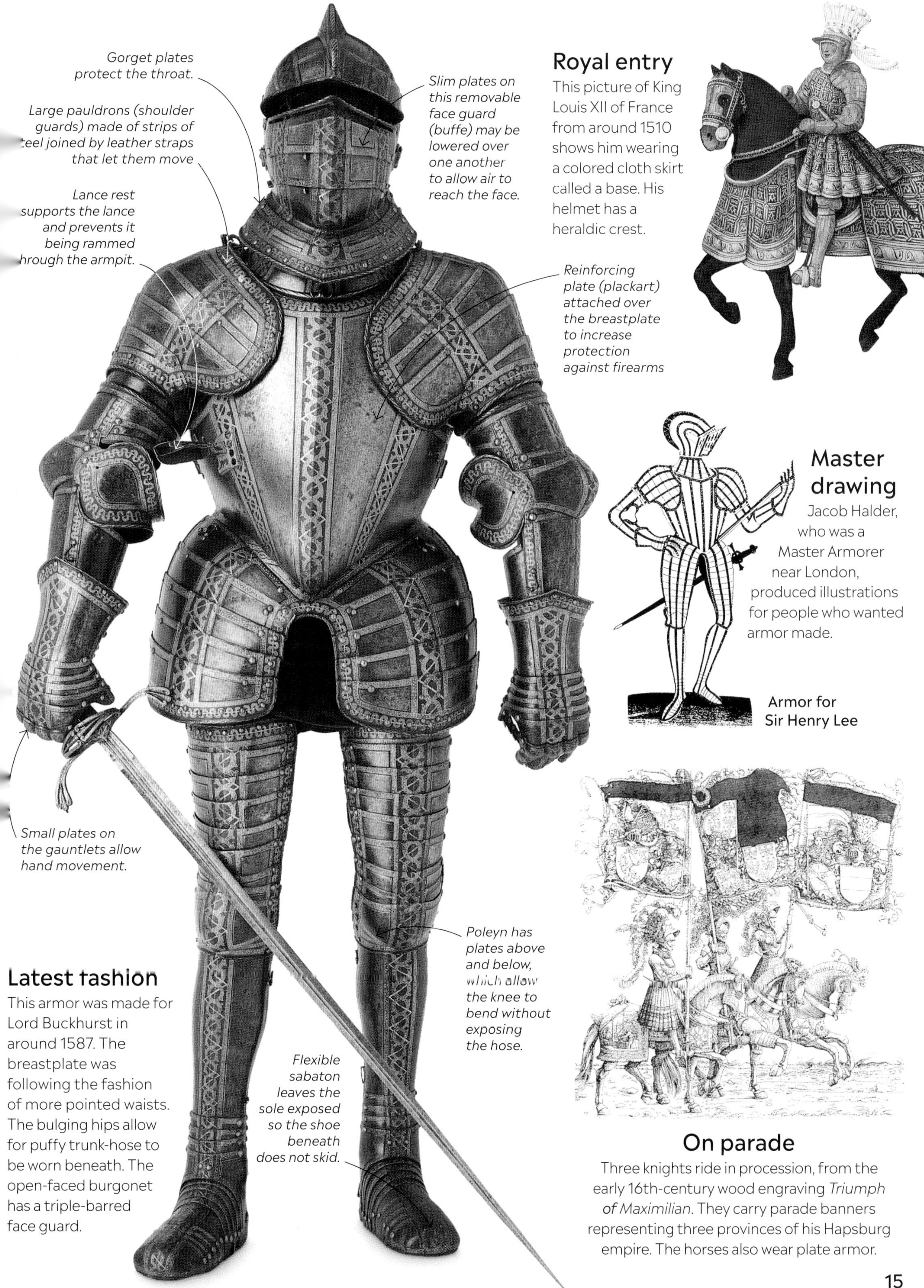
Gorget plates protect the throat.
Large pauldrons (shoulder guards) made of strips of teel joined by leather straps that let them move
Lance rest supports the lance and prevents it being rammed hrough the armpit.
Slim plates on this removable face guard (buffe) may be lowered over one another to allow air to reach the face.
Reinforcing plate (plackart) attached over the breastplate to increase protection against firearms
Small plates on the gauntlets allow hand movement.
Poleyn has plates above and below, which allow the knee to bend without exposing the hose.
Flexible sabaton leaves the sole exposed so the shoe beneath does not skid.

Royal entry

This picture of King Louis XII of France from around 1510 shows him wearing a colored cloth skirt called a base. His helmet has a heraldic crest.

Master drawing

Jacob Halder, who was a Master Armorer near London, produced illustrations for people who wanted armor made.

Armor for Sir Henry Lee

Latest fashion

This armor was made for Lord Buckhurst in around 1587. The breastplate was following the fashion of more pointed waists. The bulging hips allow for puffy trunk-hose to be worn beneath. The open-faced burgonet has a triple-barred face guard.

On parade

Three knights ride in procession, from the early 16th-century wood engraving *Triumph of Maximilian*. They carry parade banners representing three provinces of his Hapsburg empire. The horses also wear plate armor.

Inside the **armor**

A man in armor could do just about anything that a man can do when not wearing it. Some plates were attached to each other with a rivet, which allowed the two parts to pivot at that point. Others were joined by a sliding rivet, so the two plates could move in and out. Tubular-shaped plates could also have a sticking-up, or flanged, edge to fit inside the edge of another tubular plate (turner) so they could twist around.

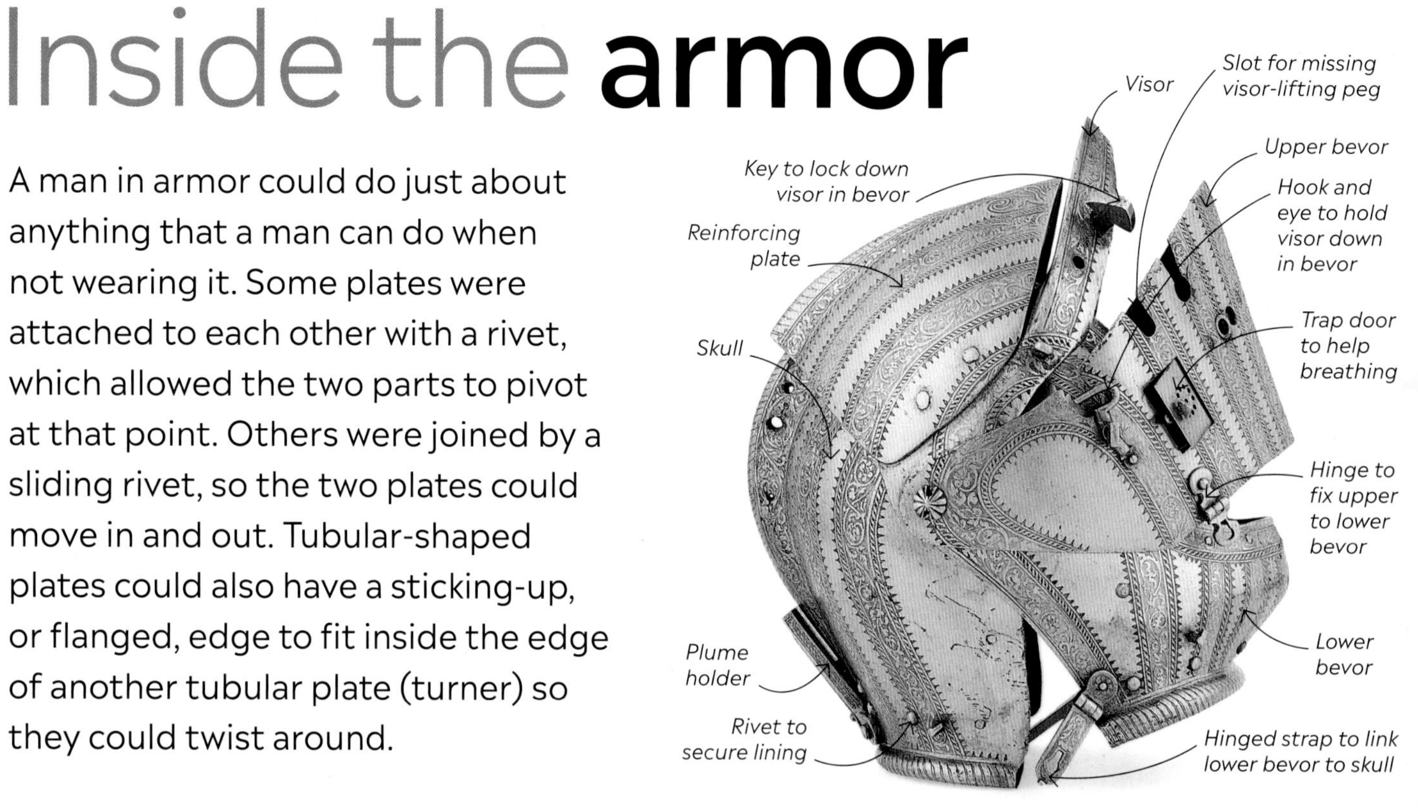

Close helmet for the til

This Italian helmet from around 1560 has reinforcing plate riveted to the skull. The visor fit inside the bevor, which is divided into two parts

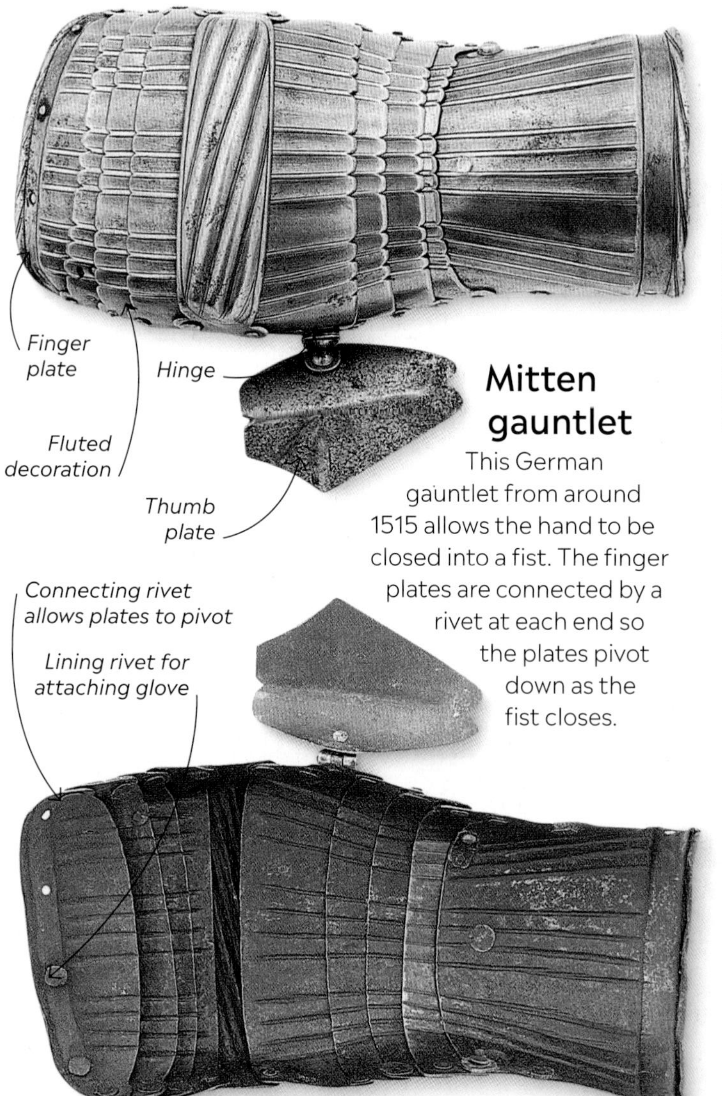

Mitten gauntlet

This German gauntlet from around 1515 allows the hand to be closed into a fist. The finger plates are connected by a rivet at each end so the plates pivot down as the fist closes.

Hot work

An armorer has heated a piece of metal in a furnace to soften it and is hammering it into shape.

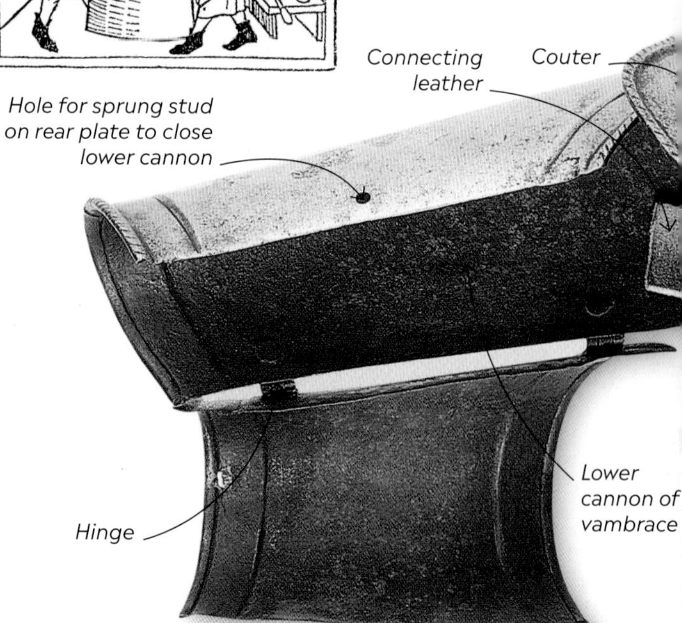

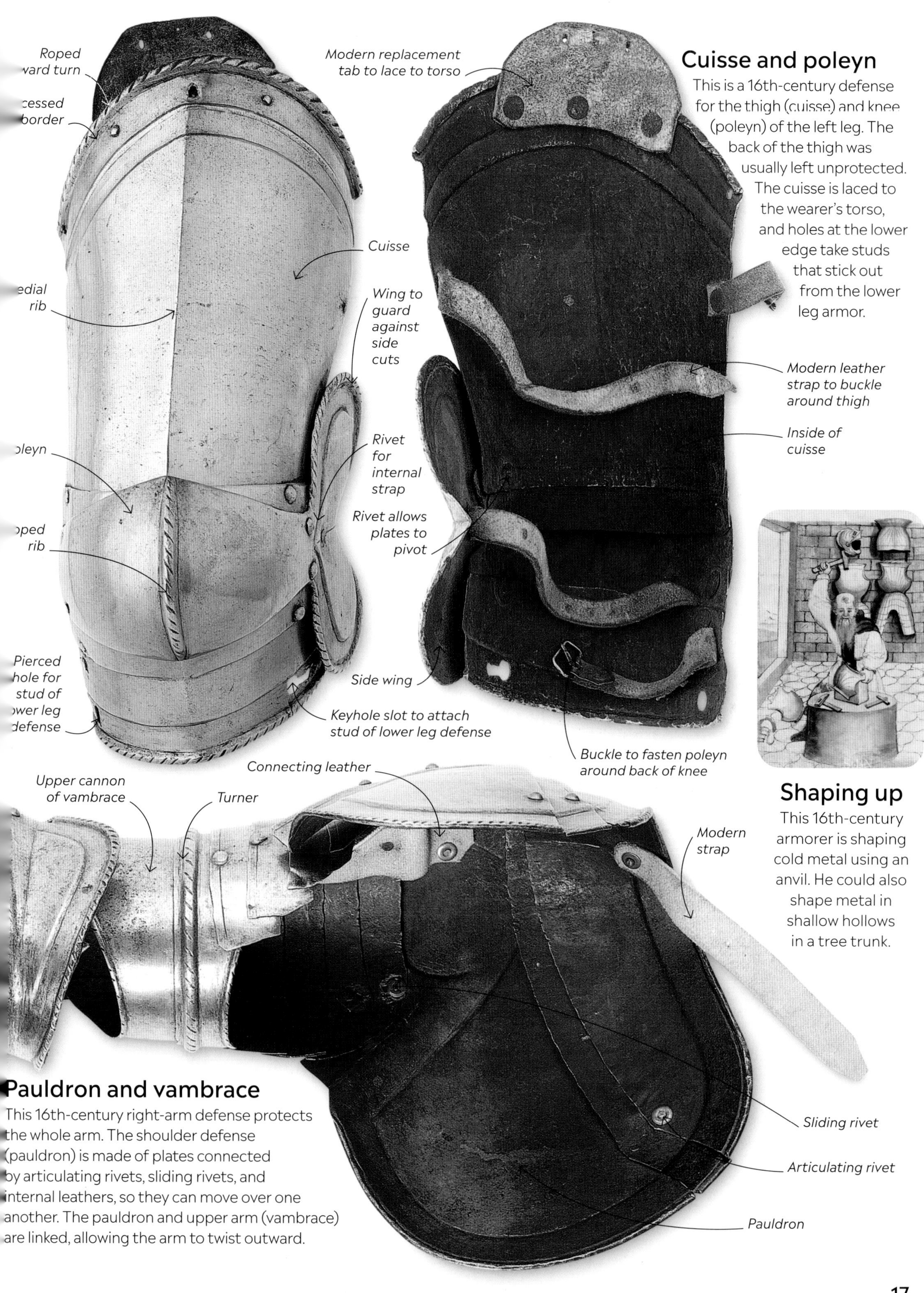

Cuisse and poleyn

This is a 16th-century defense for the thigh (cuisse) and knee (poleyn) of the left leg. The back of the thigh was usually left unprotected. The cuisse is laced to the wearer's torso, and holes at the lower edge take studs that stick out from the lower leg armor.

Shaping up

This 16th-century armorer is shaping cold metal using an anvil. He could also shape metal in shallow hollows in a tree trunk.

Pauldron and vambrace

This 16th-century right-arm defense protects the whole arm. The shoulder defense (pauldron) is made of plates connected by articulating rivets, sliding rivets, and internal leathers, so they can move over one another. The pauldron and upper arm (vambrace) are linked, allowing the arm to twist outward.

Arms and **the man**

The sword was the most important knightly weapon. As plate armor became common, pointed swords became more popular than the double-edged cutting sword because they were better for thrusting through the gaps between plates. The mace was also popular, as was the lance. Other weapons, such as the short ax and war hammer, could be used on horseback, while long-handled staff weapons, held in both hands, could be used on foot.

EYEWITNESS

Hans Talhoffer
Swordsman Hans Talhoffer (c. 1410–c. 1485) served as Master of Arms to several aristocrats in the Holy Roman Empire. He wrote books on fighting techniques, particularly judicial combats, which were used to decide an accused person's guilt.

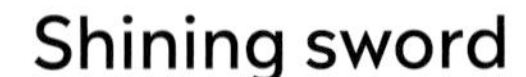

Shining sword

This late 15th-century sword has a modern replacement hilt.

Copper-gilt cross guard

Original fish-tail pommel

Horn grip

The couched lance

Early 14th-century knights charge with lances "couched" under their arms.

Flanged mace

Used as early as the 11th century, a flanged mace has ridges sticking out from the head to concentrate the force of the blow. This example has a bronze head mounted on a modern haft. An iron ball attached to a haft by a chain was called a flail.

Flange

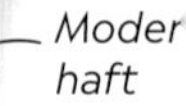

Moder haft

Maker's mark

Great sword

Two-hand swords were large versions of the ordinary sword and were swung in both hands to deliver a powerful blow. This one, possibly made in England, dates to about 1450. Large swords started to gain popularity in the 13th century.

Modern cord grip

Fish-tail pommel

Diamond-section blade

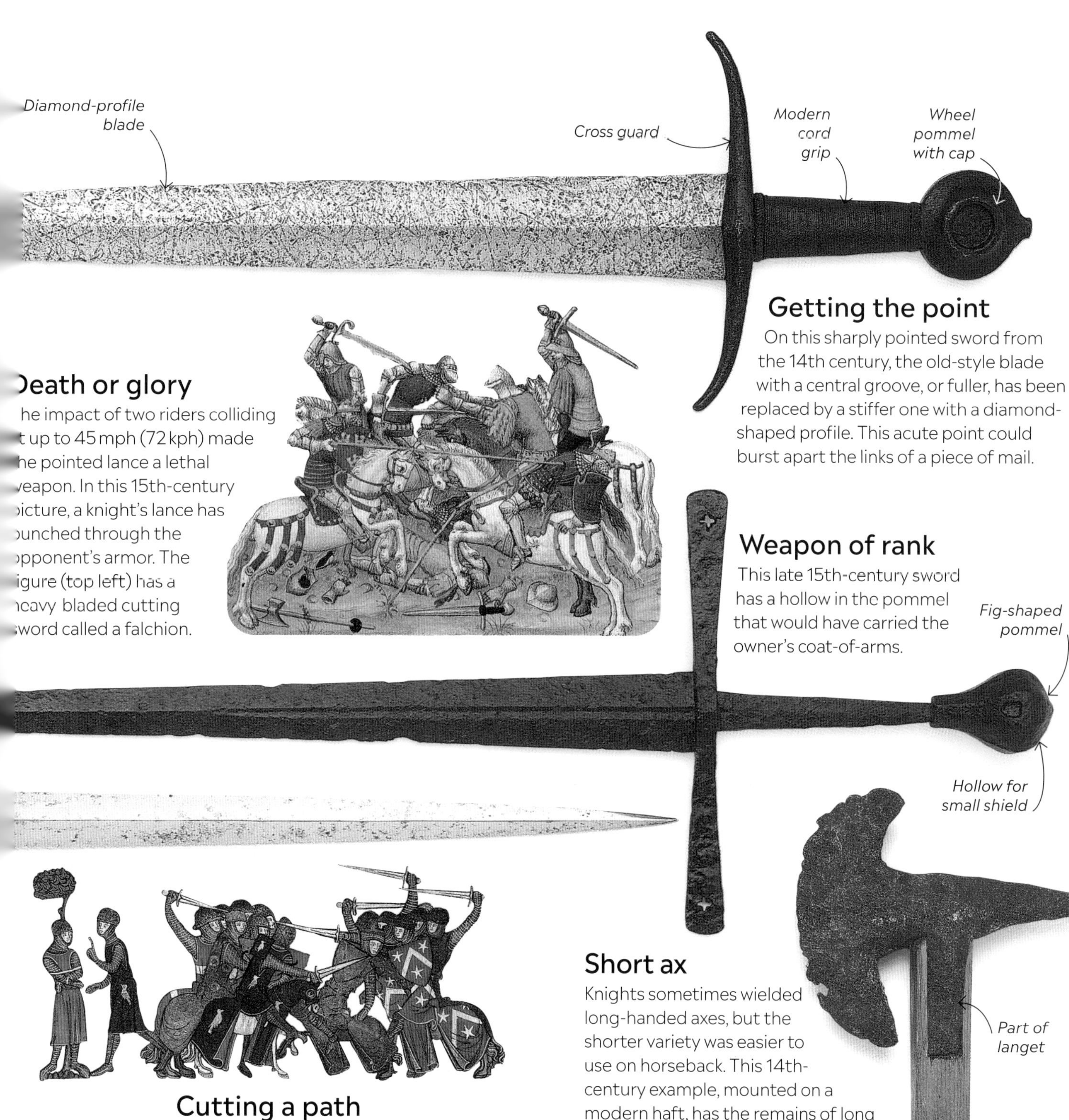

Getting the point

On this sharply pointed sword from the 14th century, the old-style blade with a central groove, or fuller, has been replaced by a stiffer one with a diamond-shaped profile. This acute point could burst apart the links of a piece of mail.

Death or glory

The impact of two riders colliding at up to 45 mph (72 kph) made the pointed lance a lethal weapon. In this 15th-century picture, a knight's lance has punched through the opponent's armor. The figure (top left) has a heavy bladed cutting sword called a falchion.

Weapon of rank

This late 15th-century sword has a hollow in the pommel that would have carried the owner's coat-of-arms.

Cutting a path

This 14th-century illustration shows pointed swords with sharp edges that could cause terrible injuries and cuts to the bones.

Short ax

Knights sometimes wielded long-handed axes, but the shorter variety was easier to use on horseback. This 14th-century example, mounted on a modern haft, has the remains of long iron langets that ran down the haft to stop the ax-head being cut off.

Single-edged blade

Rondel

Dagger

Knights did not use daggers much until the 14th century. This is a late 15th-century rondel dagger, so-called because of the protective iron disks at either end of the grip.

On horseback

Knights needed horses for warfare, jousting, hunting, traveling, and transportation. The destrier was the most expensive, often reserved for jousts. The strong, fast courser was a prized warhorse, often brough in from Italy, France, or Spain. Both horses were usually stallions. By the 13th century, most knights usually had at least two warhorses. For traveling and hunting, a well-bred, comfortable palfrey was a common choice. Squires and retainers might ride rounceys, while sumpters were used as packhorses, to carry baggage.

Fit for a king

An early 14th-century miniature shows the king of England on his warhorse. The richly decorated covering, or trapper, could be used to display heraldic arms.

Warhorse

A courser wears armor on its head, neck, and chest. The knight in this 15th-century picture wears long spurs and shows the straight-legged riding position.

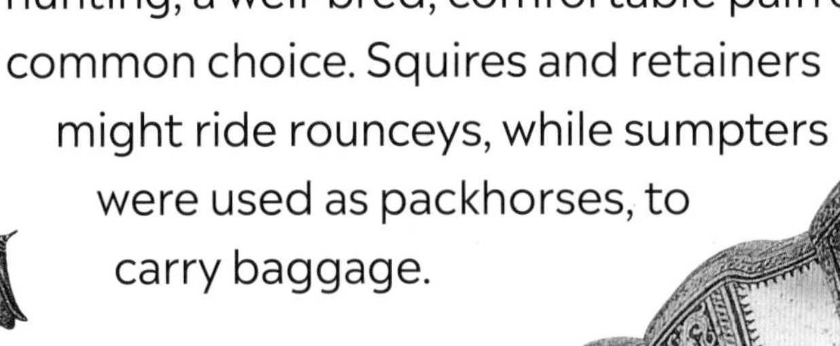

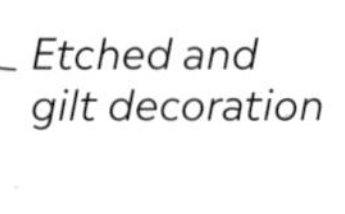

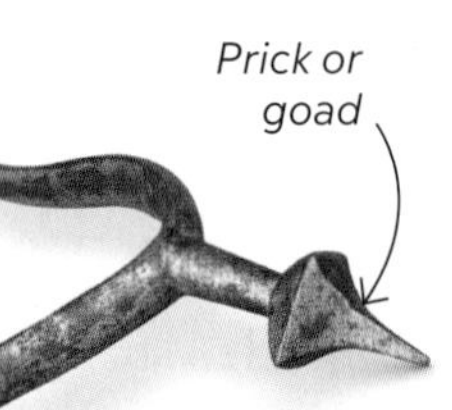

Miniature goad

A knight wore spurs on his feet. He used them to urge on his horse. This 12th- or 13th-century prick spur is made of tinned iron.

Rowel spur

Spurs with a rotating spiked rowel replaced prick spurs by the early 14th century. This spur is from the 15th century.

Firm seat

Iron stirrups like this from the 14th century were worn with straps so the knight was almost standing in them. This, together with high saddle boards, created a secure seat to fight.

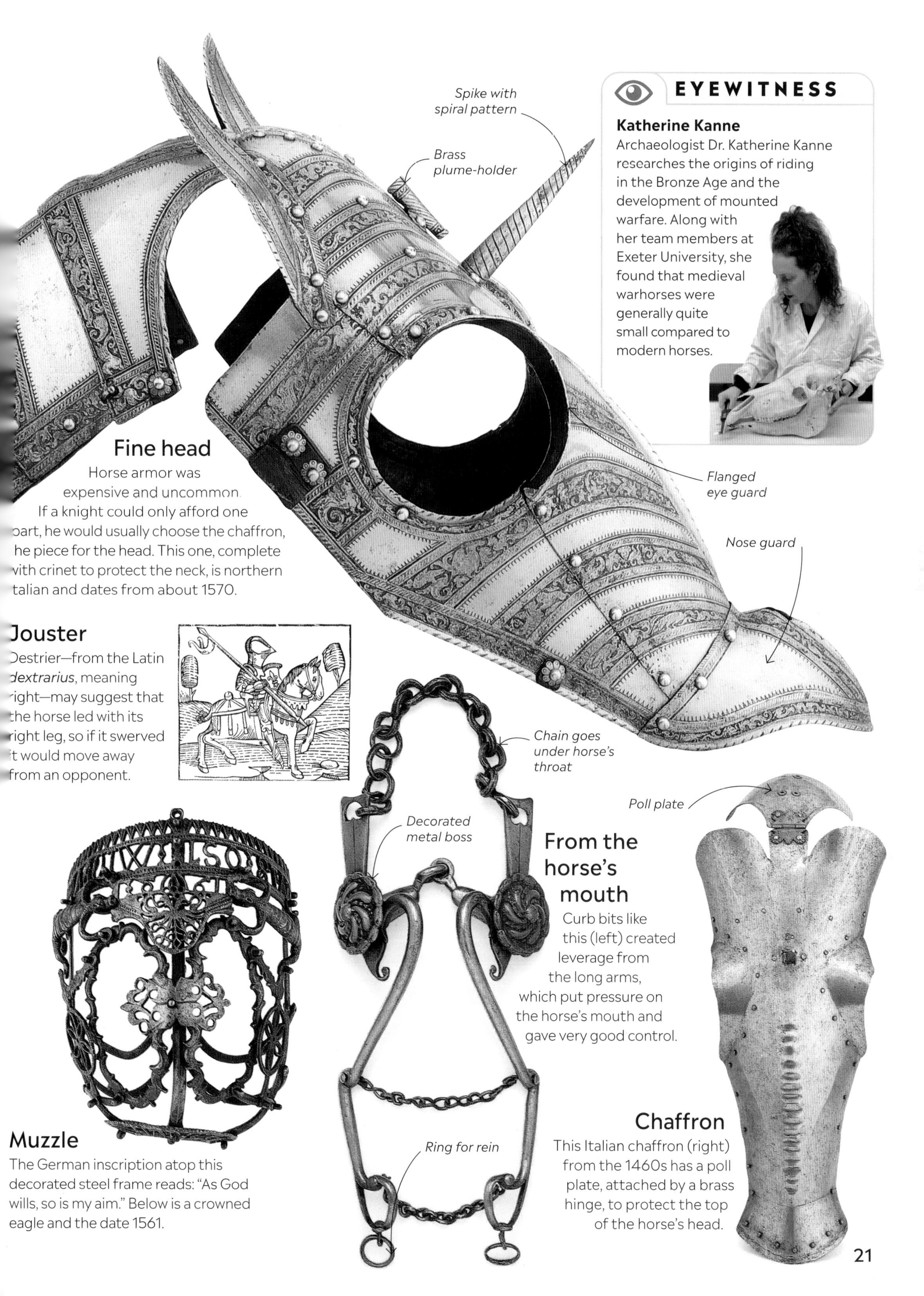

EYEWITNESS

Katherine Kanne

Archaeologist Dr. Katherine Kanne researches the origins of riding in the Bronze Age and the development of mounted warfare. Along with her team members at Exeter University, she found that medieval warhorses were generally quite small compared to modern horses.

Fine head

Horse armor was expensive and uncommon. If a knight could only afford one part, he would usually choose the chaffron, the piece for the head. This one, complete with crinet to protect the neck, is northern Italian and dates from about 1570.

Jouster

Destrier—from the Latin *dextrarius*, meaning right—may suggest that the horse led with its right leg, so if it swerved it would move away from an opponent.

From the horse's mouth

Curb bits like this (left) created leverage from the long arms, which put pressure on the horse's mouth and gave very good control.

Muzzle

The German inscription atop this decorated steel frame reads: "As God wills, so is my aim." Below is a crowned eagle and the date 1561.

Chaffron

This Italian chaffron (right) from the 1460s has a poll plate, attached by a brass hinge, to protect the top of the horse's head.

The **castle**

A castle could be a lord's home, his business headquarters, and a base for his soldiers. The first castles probably appeared in northwestern France in the ninth century, because of civil wars and Viking attacks. Although some early castles were built of stone, many consisted of earthworks and timber walls. In time, knights began to use stone, then brick, which was stronger and more fire-resistant.

Narrow slit

Windows near the ground were made small to guard against enemy missiles or soldiers climbing through. These narrow windows splayed on the inside, though, to let in light.

Motte and bailey

From the 11th century, many castles were given a mound called a motte—a last line of defense with a wooden tower on top. The courtyard, or bailey, held all the domestic buildings.

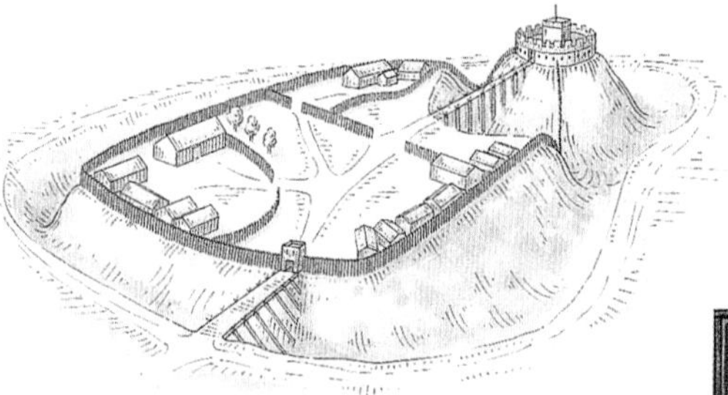

Strength in stone

The stone keep became common in the 11th and 12th centuries. The bailey was often surrounded by stone walls with square towers. Round towers appeared in the 12th century.

People at work

Stone castles cost a fortune to build and could take years to complete. The lord and the master mason chose a strong site and plan. Stone had to be brought in specially, and lime, sand, and water were needed for the mortar. The lord normally provided the materials and workforce.

Walls of defense

Concentric castles were first built in the 13th century. The inner wall was often higher so archers had a clear shot. Some old castles had outer walls added later, which gave another line of defense. Sometimes rivers were used to give broad water defenses.

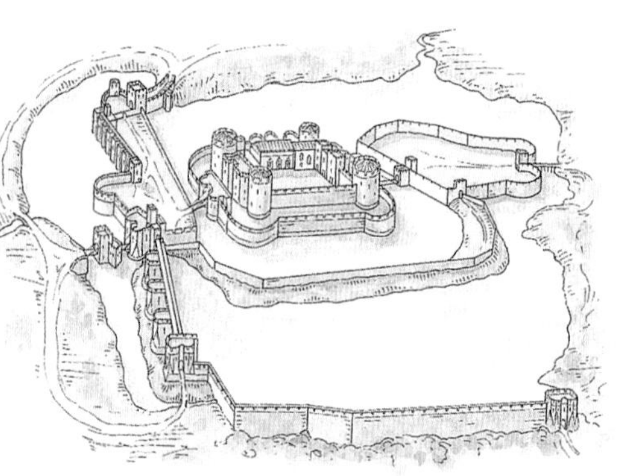

Cracking castle

Occasionally a stone tower was built on a motte, but the artificial mound was not always strong enough to take the weight. The 13th-century Clifford's Tower in York, England, has cracked as a result.

Gatehouse

At Dover, England, the castle gate is flanked by two round towers. The walls are splayed at the base—the thick masonry helps protect them against mining. The deep, dry ditch thwarts attackers.

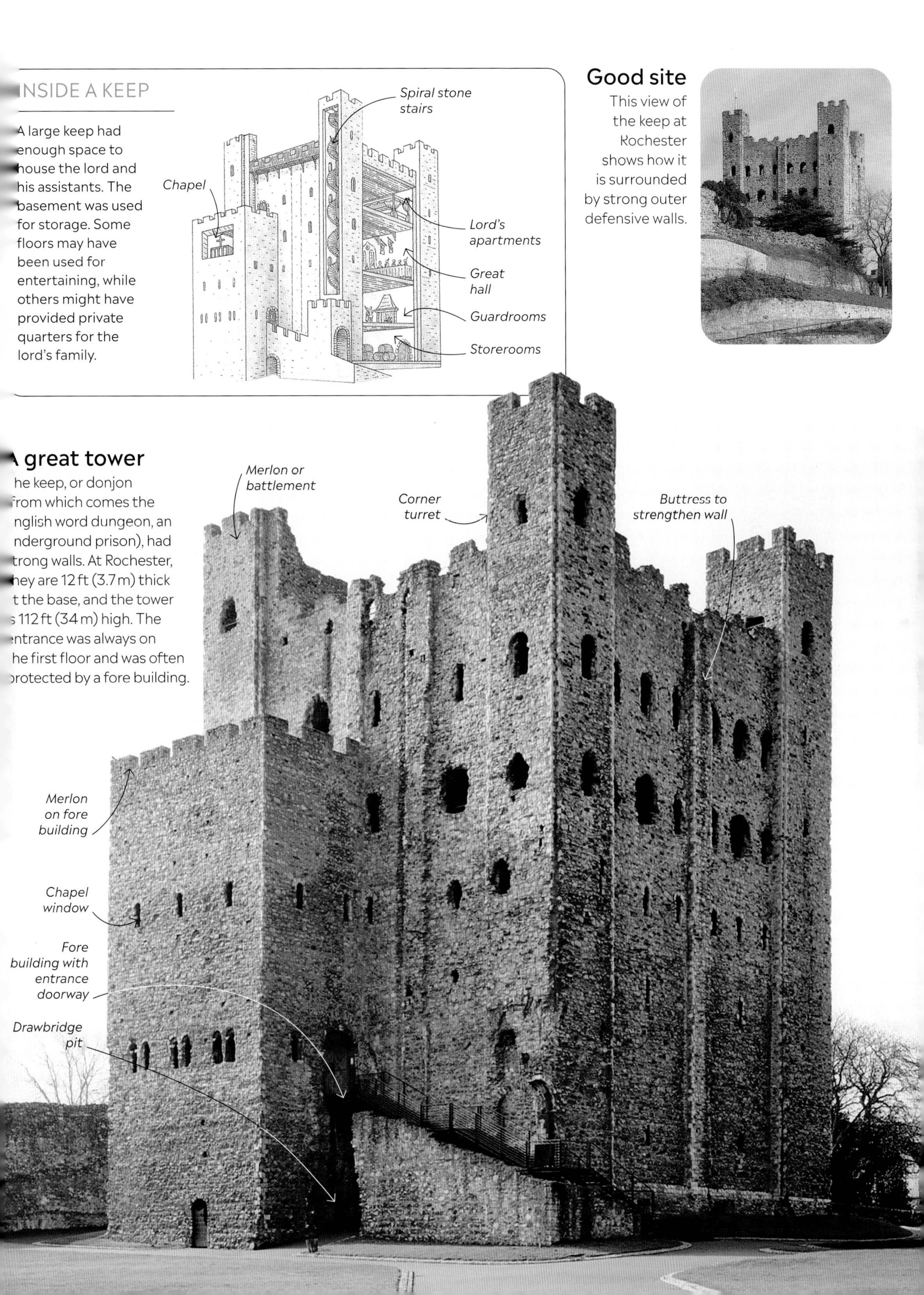

INSIDE A KEEP

A large keep had enough space to house the lord and his assistants. The basement was used for storage. Some floors may have been used for entertaining, while others might have provided private quarters for the lord's family.

Good site

This view of the keep at Rochester shows how it is surrounded by strong outer defensive walls.

\ great tower

he keep, or donjon from which comes the nglish word dungeon, an nderground prison), had trong walls. At Rochester, hey are 12 ft (3.7 m) thick t the base, and the tower s 112 ft (34 m) high. The ntrance was always on he first floor and was often rotected by a fore building.

The castle at **war**

The first obstacle for the enemy was a ditch all the way around the castle, which was sometimes filled with stakes. Moats—ditches that were filled with water—were less common: they put off attackers from burrowing under the walls. Towers jutted out from the walls so archers could shoot along the walls to repel enemies.

Wooden doors barred from behind

Gatehouse

The gatehouse was always strongl defended. Usually a wooden liftin bridge spanned the ditch and a gat called a portcullis could form a barrie

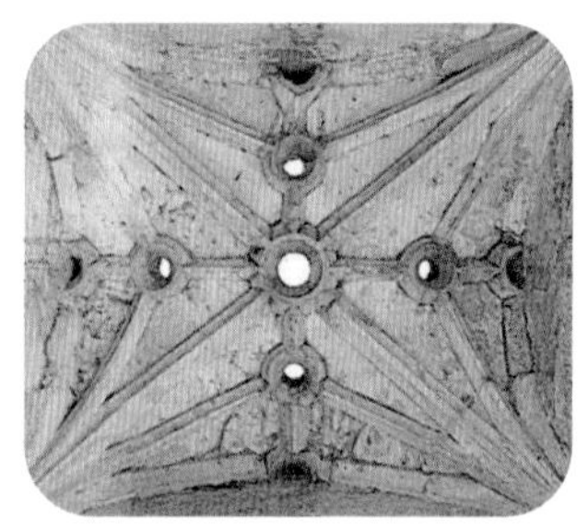

Vaulted ceiling

There are holes built into the gatehouse's ceiling. These allowed people to pour water down to put out fires or to drop boiling water or stones on attackers.

Knightly stronghold

Bodiam Castle in Sussex, England, was built in 1385 by Sir Edward Dalyngrigge amid fears of a French invasion. It has a single stone curtain wall with round towers at the corners and is surrounded by a moat to protect the occupants.

High turrets gave distant views of approaching enemies.

Machicolations along gate tower

Battlement on section of wall

Round flanking tower; the shape leaves no corners for a ram or miners

Moat

Over the walls

his 14th-century picture shows the 11th-century crusader, Godfrey of Bouillon, attacking rtifications. His men are using scaling ladders.

Embrasure

An embrasure was an alcove in the wall with a narrow opening, or "loophole," to the outside. This allowed defenders to look and shoot out without showing themselves.

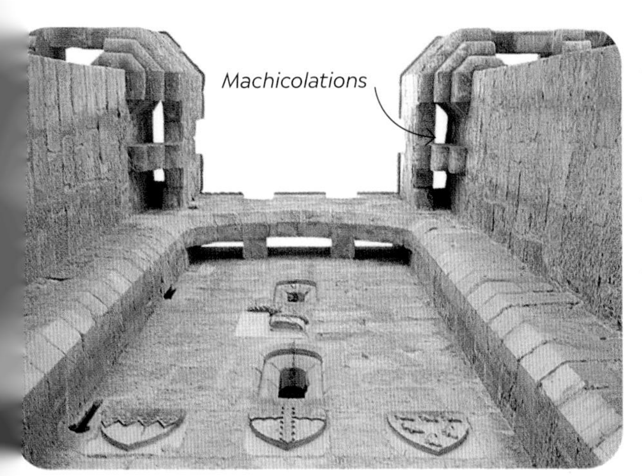

Flanking towers

This picture was taken looking up the front of the gatehouse. Flanking towers jut out on either side to protect the gate. Water poured through the machicolations could put out fires or repel enemies.

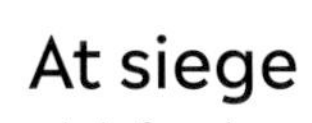

At siege

Both attackers and defenders are using siege engines (pp.26–27) to hurl missiles.

Siege **warfare**

An enemy attacking a castle would usually make a formal demand for the people inside to surrender. If this was rejected, they would try to take the castle by siege. The first way was to surround the castle and prevent anyone leaving or going in, thereby starving the defenders into submission. The second was to use force, including catapults or battering rams to break down the walls or gates.

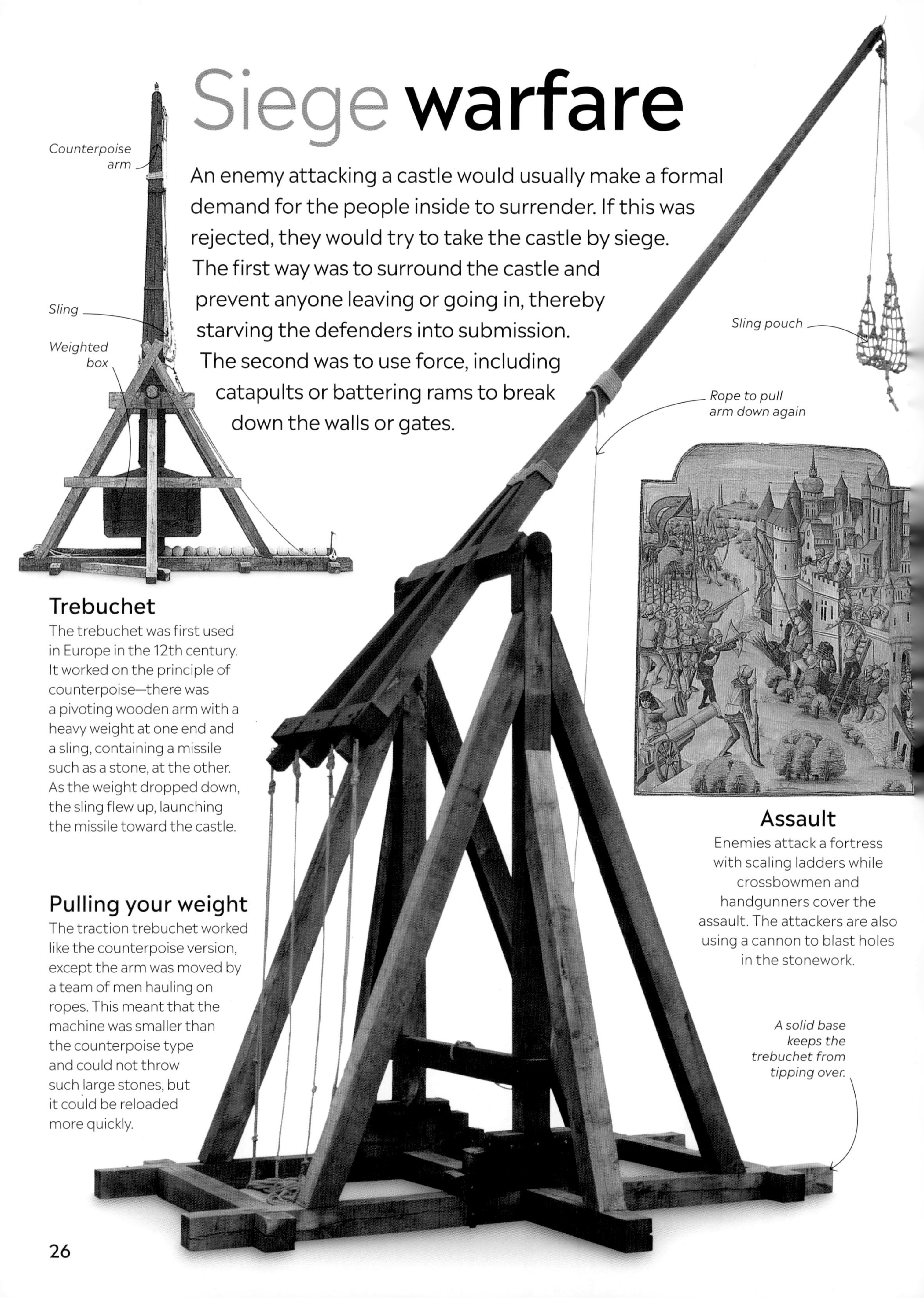

Trebuchet

The trebuchet was first used in Europe in the 12th century. It worked on the principle of counterpoise—there was a pivoting wooden arm with a heavy weight at one end and a sling, containing a missile such as a stone, at the other. As the weight dropped down, the sling flew up, launching the missile toward the castle.

Pulling your weight

The traction trebuchet worked like the counterpoise version, except the arm was moved by a team of men hauling on ropes. This meant that the machine was smaller than the counterpoise type and could not throw such large stones, but it could be reloaded more quickly.

Assault

Enemies attack a fortress with scaling ladders while crossbowmen and handgunners cover the assault. The attackers are also using a cannon to blast holes in the stonework.

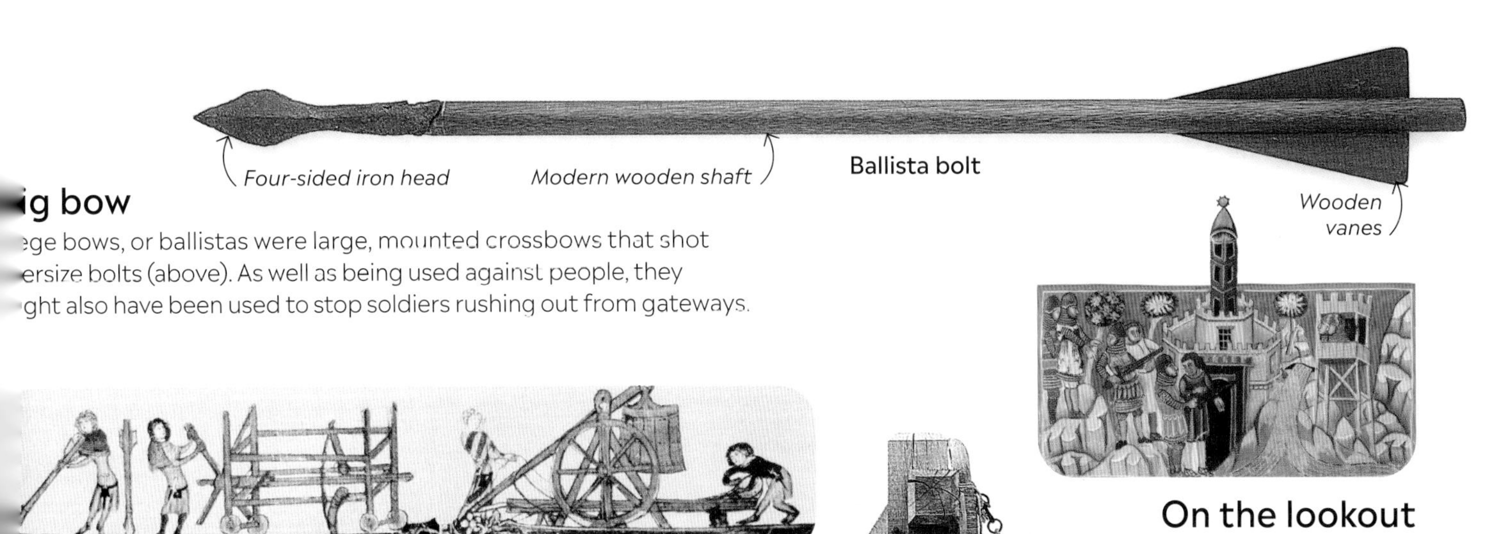

Ballista bolt

ig bow

:ge bows, or ballistas were large, mounted crossbows that shot ersize bolts (above). As well as being used against people, they ght also have been used to stop soldiers rushing out from gateways.

allista and trebuchet

is illustration from the 14th-century *Romance of lexander* shows a ballista with a winch worked by a rew thread to pull back both slider and bowstring.

On the lookout

In this illustration of a siege, the attackers are using a tall wooden tower as a lookout post.

Hundreds of horse-drawn wagons transported the machines and ammunition o the site of a siege.

Surrender

This 15th-century illustration shows the defenders formally surrendering. If taken after a siege, a town or castle was occasionally looted by the soldiers since its occupants had refused to give up upon request.

Side view of catapult

Front view of catapult

Catapult in use

Pulling power

This catapult used the pulling power of a skein of twisted ropes, sinews, or even hair to force the arm up against a bar. When winched back and released, the arm flew up, launching its missile from a wooden cup.

Armed to **fight**

Arming doublet

Mail gusset

Waxed points

Early armor was quite easy to put on. Mail was pulled on over the head, while a coat-of-plates (pp.12–13) was buckled at the back, or sides and shoulders. Plate armor was more complicated to put on, but a squire could arm a knight in a few minutes, and the armor could be speedily removed if necessary. Here a squire is arming a knight in late 15th-century German Gothic-style armor.

1 Arming doublet

This padded garment has waxed points to fasten different parts of the armor. The mail gussets cover the gaps that will be left by the plates.

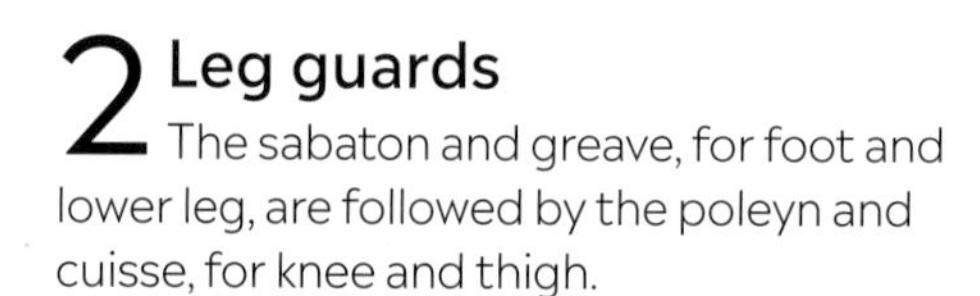

2 Leg guards

The sabaton and greave, for foot and lower leg, are followed by the poleyn and cuisse, for knee and thigh.

3 Mail skirt

Mail around the waist protects the groin, which is not fully covered by the plates. Flexible mail here allows the knight to bend or sit.

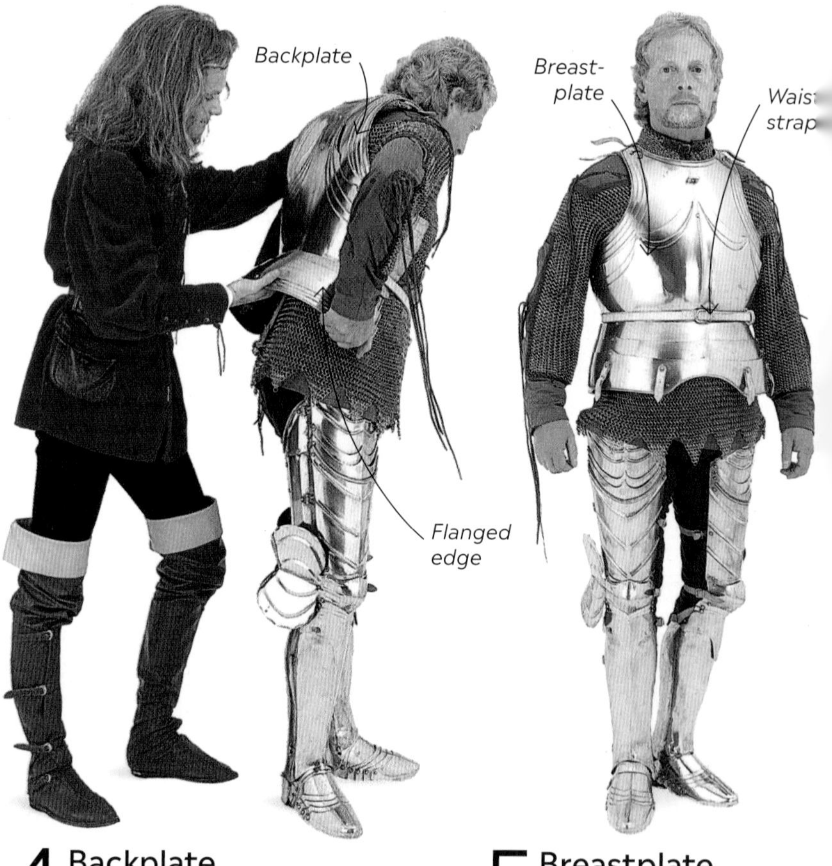

4 Backplate

The backplate is lifted into position. It has an angled lower edge to deflect weapons from the buttocks and legs.

5 Breastplate

Breast and back together are called the cuirass. They are secured by the waist straps and are joined at the shoulders.

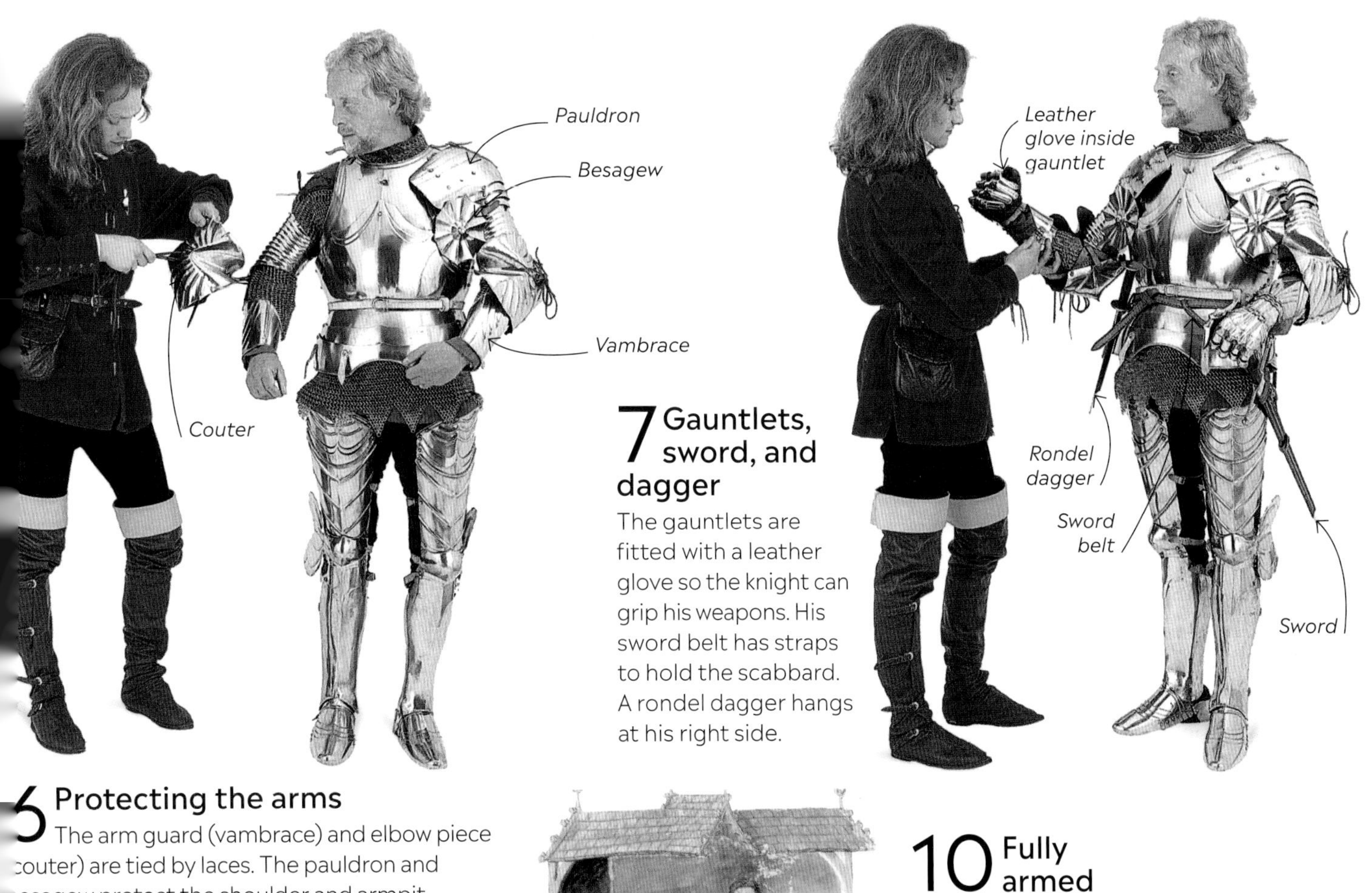

7 Gauntlets, sword, and dagger

The gauntlets are fitted with a leather glove so the knight can grip his weapons. His sword belt has straps to hold the scabbard. A rondel dagger hangs at his right side.

6 Protecting the arms

The arm guard (vambrace) and elbow piece couter) are tied by laces. The pauldron and besagew protect the shoulder and armpit.

Arming a knight

A rare picture from around 1450 shows a knight being armed for foot combat.

8 Bevor

A chin defense, or bevor, protects the lower half of the face when wearing the sallet, a helmet popular in western Europe.

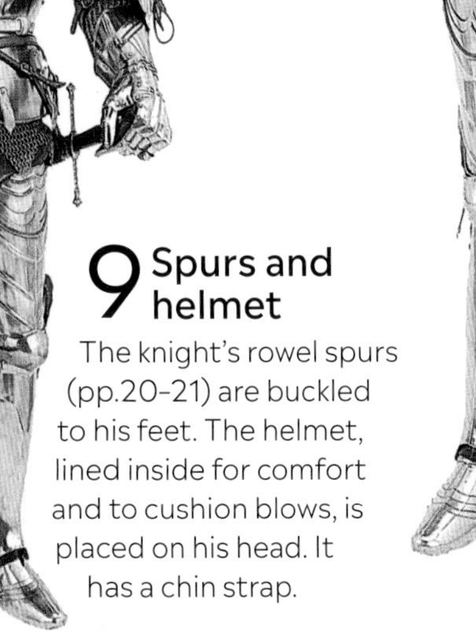

9 Spurs and helmet

The knight's rowel spurs (pp.20–21) are buckled to his feet. The helmet, lined inside for comfort and to cushion blows, is placed on his head. It has a chin strap.

10 Fully armed

The knight holds a mace. Armed from head to foot (or cap-a-pie), he is ready to mount his warhorse.

Mace

The enemy

Knights soon found themselves facing dangerous enemies. The English axmen at Hastings in 1066 cut down Norman knights, while Scottish spear formations stopped cavalry charges at Bannockburn in 1314, a strategy also favored by the Swiss, who used pikes. Different types of bow were highly effective against mounted knights. In early 15th-century Bohemia (now part of Czechia) the Hussites blasted German knights, using the first massed guns.

The longbow

This type of bow was usually made of a stave of yew wood about the height of the archer. It was fitted with horn nocks at the tips to take the hemp string. War bows probably needed a pull of at least 80 lb (36 kg), and many were far more powerful.

Barbed arrow-head

Leather bracer

Stave of yew wood

Horn nock to take string

Arrows placed in front for quick reloading

Slinger

Some infantrymen used slings. The stone or lead bullets were lethal if they struck a person in the face, but they could not damage armor. Sometimes a sling was attached to a wooden handle to increase range.

A bristling hedge

Cavalrymen were unhappy about forcing their horses against spears or pikes; infantry in close formation with a "hedge" of these weapons could hold off mounted knights.

An archer

Longbows were used in many European countries, although on the mainland the crossbow was more popular. The string of the longbow was brought back between the cheek and the ear. The leather bracer protected the bow arm from an accidental slap from the string; a leather tab protected the drawing fingers. Archers wore various pieces of defensive armor, or just a padded doublet (left).

At the butts

Archers needed constant practice to maintain their skills. In this 14th-century picture, English archers shoot at the butts—targets set up on earthen mounds.

The goose feather

Fletchings, or feather flights, make the arrow spin for a truer flight. Usually goose feathers were used for the arrows.

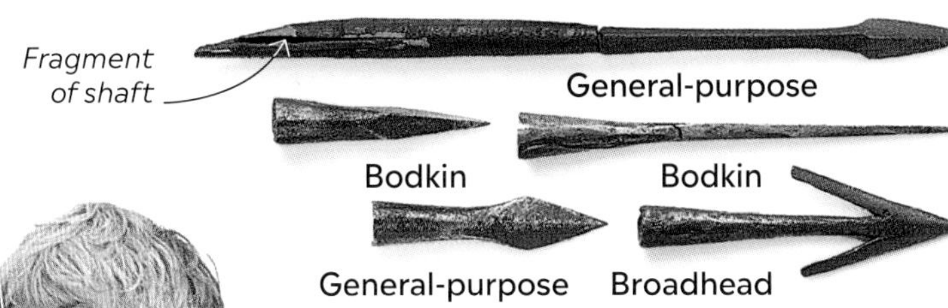

Arrowheads

Depending on their use, arrowheads had various shapes. Broadheads were barbed for use against animals, while bodkins were for penetrating armor.

Long-range fighting

Arrows from a longbow could probably reach a distance of about 980 ft (300 m), so could be dropped on an advancing enemy. This was done by shooting the arrows upward. Bodkins could punch through mail links, and cavalry horses were also vulnerable.

Welsh archer

From the 12th century, English armies employed Welsh longbowmen. In this crude picture, the rough bow is shown far too small. The bare foot may be to give a better grip.

Longbow versus crossbow

A skilled archer (such as the men in the center of this 15th-century illustration) might release 12 arrows per minute. A crossbowman (on the left) could only shoot two in this time, but these would penetrate deeply.

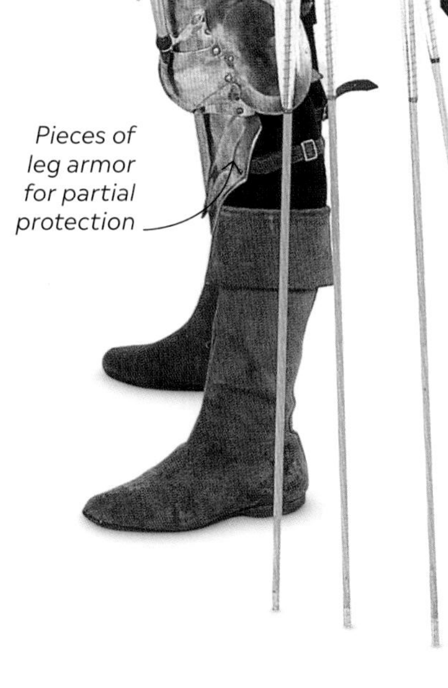

Keen eye

An archer carried 24 arrows, known as a sheaf. Additional arrows were supplied by wagon. Archers would often stick their arrows into the ground in front of them, so they were ready to be shot quickly.

Into **battle**

The rules of chivalry dictated that knights should show courtesy to defeated enemies, but this code was not always observed. Knights often showed little mercy to foot soldiers, cutting them down ruthlessly in pursuit. Much was at stake in a battle—defeat might mean the loss of an army or even a throne. So commanders preferred to raid enemy territory, which brought extra supplies as well as destroying property.

Shock of battle

This 15th-century picture shows the crash of two opposing cavalry forces in full plate armor. Those struck down by lances in the first line, even if only slightly wounded, were liable to be trampled by the horses of either the enemy or of their own knights following behind.

One spike always points upward.

Caltrops

Only an inch or so high, iron-made caltrops were scattered over the battleground to lame horses or men from the opposing army who accidentally trod on them. When thrown, they always landed with one spike pointing upward.

Three spikes rest on the ground.

Warrior kings

Many medieval kings were shown on their great seal as head of their army, on horseback and wearing full armor. Here Henry I, King of England from 1100–1135 and Duke of Normandy, wears a mail coat and conical helmet.

In pursuit

This 13th-century battle scene shows one force pursuing the opposing side. Often the pursuers did not hesitate to strike at men with their backs turned. However, breaking ranks to chase the enemy could put the rest of your army in danger.

Fighting on foot

Although knights were trained as horsemen, it was often thought better for a large part of an army to dismount and form a solid body, often supported by archers and groups of cavalry. This 14th-century illustration shows a clash between the royal army of France and rebels from the County of Flanders in the Battle of Courtrai in 1302.

Tall Italian town family tower

The couched lance

By the 12th century, rather than using lances to stab or throw, galloping mounted knights preferred tucking ("couching") them under their arm to increase the force of the blow. This ivory chess piece of about 1130 shows two knights with couched lances.

Spoils of war

Victors would often capture the defeated army's baggage, which could contain many valuables, especially if the ousted leader was a prince. In this 14th-century Italian picture, the victors are examining the spoils.

Castle **life**

The castle did not just house a garrison, it was home for the knight and his household. Everyone had their meals in the great hall; estate business was also done here. There was also a kitchen (often a separate building in case of fire), a chapel, an armorer's workshop, a smithy, stables, kennels, pens for animals, a water supply—such as a well—and large storerooms to keep the castle well stocked.

Song and dance

Music often accompanied meals. Dances usually involved many people who held hands in various types of ring dance.

Wall sconce

This gilt-copper 16th-century wa sconce for burning candles bear the Castelnau-LaLoubère family' coat of arms, encircled by the collar of the Order of St. Michael

The lord's table

On this 1316 manuscript, Lancelot tells King Arthur and the whole household gathered in the great hall of his adventures.

Silver cruet

This 14th-century silver vessel was kept in a chapel to hold the holy water or wine used at Mass.

Spiked

This chapel candlestick, dating to around 1230, had a long spike to take the candle.

A game of chess

Duke Francis of Angoulême (later king of France) plays chess with his sister Marguerite in a picture from around 1504. Being a war game, chess was popular with knights.

Blazing fire

Large fireplaces could be set in the thick stone walls of castles.

Hand basin

Pairs of basins like this, called gemellions, were used to wash people's hands at the table. A helper would pour water over the person's hands from one basin into the other, then dry the hands with a towel.

A knight kneels before his lady.

Chamber pot

Although richer people might use chamber pots like this, castles often had lavatories built into the walls. A chute sent human waste beyond the castle wall.

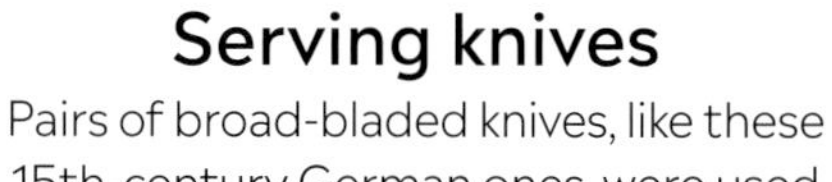

Serving knives

Pairs of broad-bladed knives, like these 15th-century German ones, were used for serving food. The leather sheath has lost its cap.

Steelyard weight

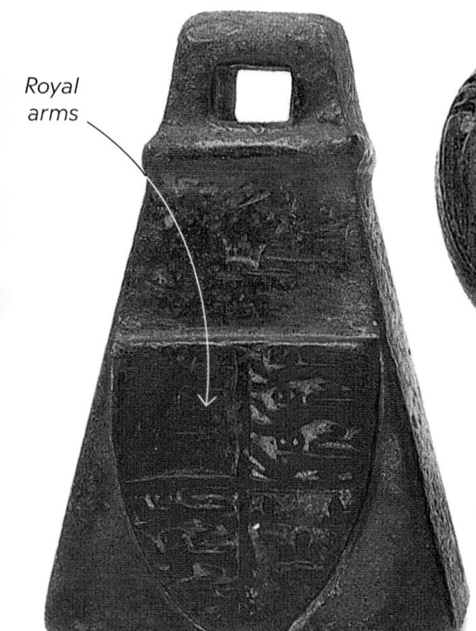

Bronze weights

This 13th-century steelyard weight was hung from a pivoting metal arm to work out the weight of an object placed on the other end.

Each guest brought their own personal knife to castle banquets.

Manor **lords**

Some knights were mercenary soldiers who fought for money. Others, particularly until the 13th century, lived at their lord's expense as household troops in his castle. Increasingly, many were given pieces of land by their lord. Such men became lords of the manor and lived off its produce. The lord held a large part of the manor and "his" peasants—workers of varying status—owed him service in return for their homes.

Home defense

Stokesay is a fortified manor house in Shropshire, England. Built mostly in the 13th century, it consists of a hall and chamber block with a tower at each end.

All in the game

This wealthy 13th-century couple play chess. Other popular board games were checkers and backgammon.

My seal on it

Noblemen were often illiterate, so they used a wax seal to validate documents. This is Robert FitzWalter's seal; he made King John agree to the Magna Carta in 1215.

Ivory chess pieces

These 12th-century Scandinavian chess pieces are carved from walrus ivory.

phill struggle

edieval peasants grew d harvested crops. This th-century picture shows asants coaxing a hay rt up a steep slope.

Garden of delight

In this 15th-century manor, one ouse has a frame of timber filled in with wattle and daub (mud or clay). Close by is an orchard of fruit trees.

ike father, like son

nese details from a 15th-century tar show a praying knight with his ns. The eldest son would become knight; his daughters would hope marry noblemen. Younger ildren often went into the church.

Domed lid

Decorated casket

This large casket belonged to a wealthy 15th-century family. It is made of wood covered in bone panels carved with biblical scenes.

A 15th-century nobleman would often wear a short, padded jacket.

The lord

The status and rank of a lord varied. Some were powerful men who held a number of manors. A bailiff would look after the estates when the lord was away. He might visit a town to meet trade merchants or to borrow money from money-lenders.

Manor ladies

In the Middle Ages, women, even those o
noble rank, had fewer rights than wome
today. Many women had an arrange
marriage by the age of 14. But the lady wa
her husband's equal in private life. She coul
support her husband and take responsibilit
for the castle when he was away. She migh
even have to defend the castle in he
husband's absence if it was besiege
and hold it against her enemies

The life of the lady

The lady ruled the kitchens and living quarters. She had officials to run the household affairs, but she checked all the accounts and agreed to any expenses. She also received guests and arranged for their accommodation. Ladies-in-waiting were her friends, maidservants attended her, and nurses looked after her children.

Women of accomplishment

Some women could read and write, and speak foreign languages. In this picture, ladies with books represent Philosophy and the Liberal Arts.

A modern sculpture of Nicola de la Haye at Lincoln Castle

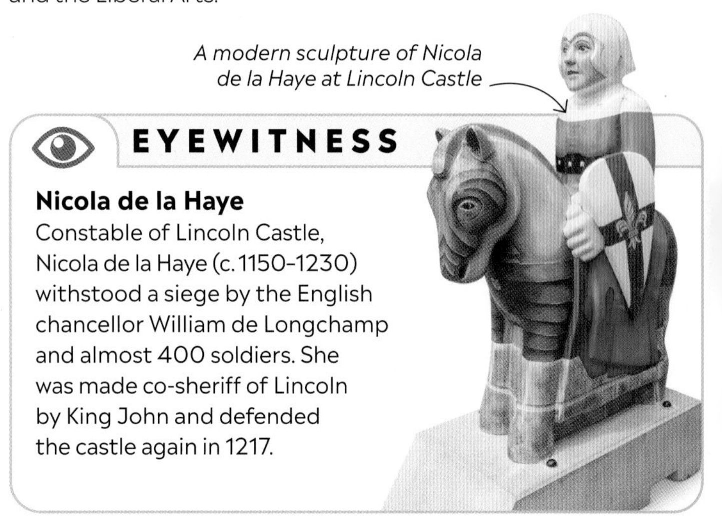

EYEWITNESS

Nicola de la Haye

Constable of Lincoln Castle, Nicola de la Haye (c. 1150–1230) withstood a siege by the English chancellor William de Longchamp and almost 400 soldiers. She was made co-sheriff of Lincoln by King John and defended the castle again in 1217.

:leanor of Aquitaine

ne of the most powerful women f her time, Eleanor (c. 1122–1204) narried King Louis VII of France and oined him on crusades. She then ivorced Louis to marry the future ing Henry II of England. Mother o two English kings, Richard I nd John, she was imprisoned or plotting against Henry. She ater became regent of England.

Bad news

A lady swoons on hearing of her husband's death. Marriages were arranged by the couples' families, but a husband and wife could grow to love one another.

Flemish gold brooch

Jewels

Women liked to display their rank with rings and brooches. The 15th-century brooch at the top is probably Flemish and depicts a woman; the 14th-century English brooch is decorated with coiled monsters.

“Suitable” jobs

Some men thought teaching women to read was dangerous. In this 15th-century picture, one woman spins woolen thread while another combs out the wool.

On bended knees

A knight places nis hands in those of the lady. He is ndicating that he will serve her—an deal of courtly love that was not borne out n practice.

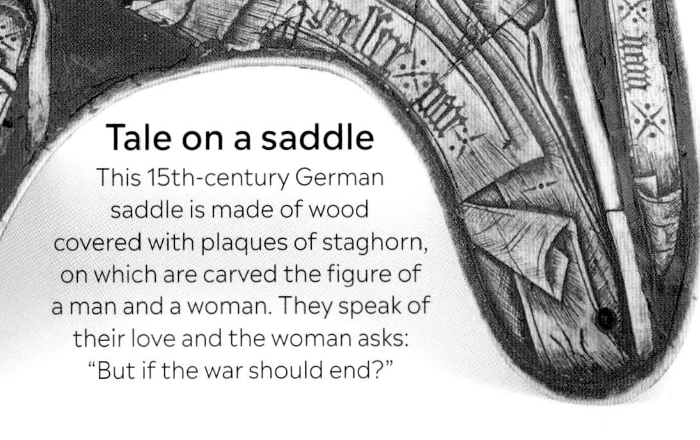

Tale on a saddle

This 15th-century German saddle is made of wood covered with plaques of staghorn, on which are carved the figure of a man and a woman. They speak of their love and the woman asks: “But if the war should end?”

Sidesaddle

Noblewomen were often active hunters. This medallion from 1477 shows Mary of Burgundy carrying her hawk and riding sidesaddle, which solved the difficulty of sitting on a horse in a long dress but was more difficult than riding astride.

The ideal of **chivalry**

The word "chivalry" comes from *cheval,* French for horse, reflecting the horsemanship of early knights. Often, they treated enemy knights well because they were of equal rank; this evolved into a knightly code of conduct. Influenced by French troubadours, the code also emphasized courtly manners toward women. Books on chivalry appeared, though knights often found it hard to live up to the ideal.

True-love knots

Medallions sometimes marked special occasions. This one commemorates the marriage of Margaret of Austria to the Duke of Savoy in 1501.

Knight in shining armor

This 15th-century shield shows a knight kneeling before his lady. The words on the scroll mean "You or death."

What's in a name?

This 15th-century book *The Lovelorn Heart* illustrates how people in medieval romance often stood for objects or feelings. Here a knight reads an inscription while his companion, Desire, lies sleeping.

Sir Lancelot and Guinevere

King Arthur was possibly a fifth-century warrior, but the legends of the king and the knights of the round table gained popularity in 13th-century Europe. They tell of the love between Arthur's queen, Guinevere, and Sir Lancelot. Here, Sir Lancelot crosses the sword bridge to rescue Guinevere.

The knight of the cart

This illustration shows Lancelot meeting a dwarf who offers to tell him where Guinevere is if he will ride in the cart. It was thought a disgrace for a knight to travel in a cart, which was how condemned criminals were sent to their execution.

Royal champion

Sir Edward Dymoke was the champion of Queen Elizabeth I of England. At her coronation banquet, it was his job to ride fully armed into the hall and hurl his gauntlet to the ground to defy anyone who wished to question the queen's right to rule. This challenge was made at every coronation until that of George IV in 1821.

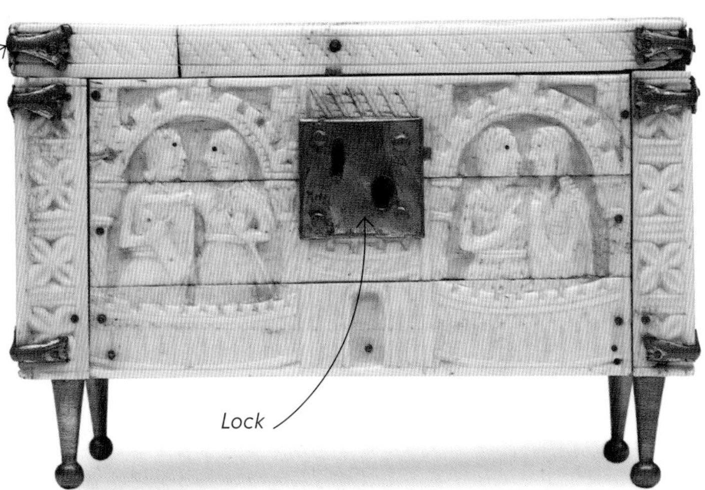

Tragic lovers

This 12th-century box tells the tale of the knight Tristan, who drank a love potion and fell in love with Iseult, the bride of King Mark, Tristan's uncle.

The tournament

Fighting men have always trained for battle. Tournaments probably started in the 11th century as practice for war in which two teams of knights fought a mock battle, called a tourney or mêlée. Defeated knights gave up their horse and armor to the victor. Other contests, such as jousts, also appeared. In the 17th century, the tournament was replaced in most countries by displays of horsemanship, called carousels.

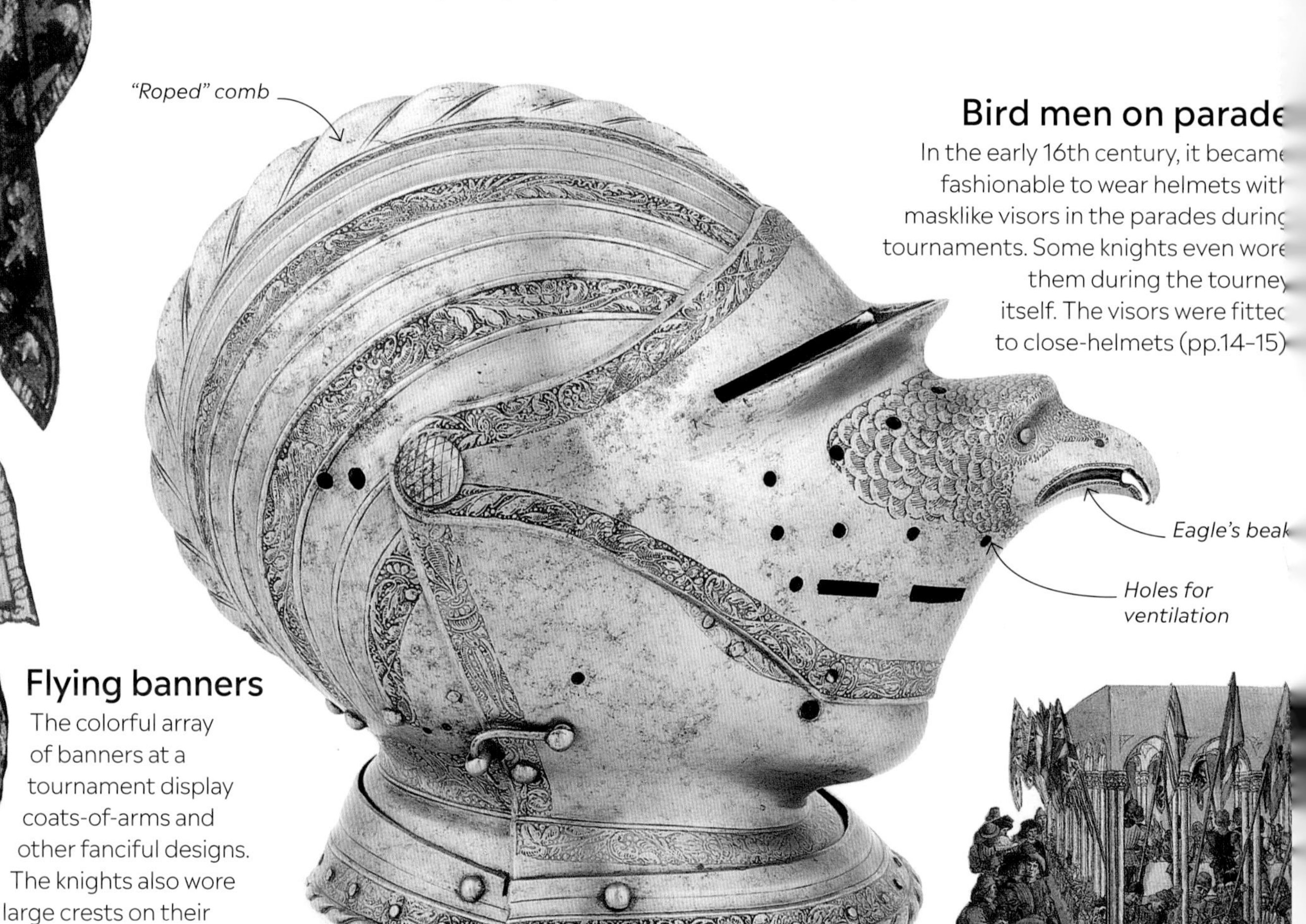

Bird men on parade

In the early 16th century, it became fashionable to wear helmets with masklike visors in the parades during tournaments. Some knights even wore them during the tourney itself. The visors were fitted to close-helmets (pp.14–15).

Flying banners

The colorful array of banners at a tournament display coats-of-arms and other fanciful designs. The knights also wore large crests on their helms, even though these were no longer worn in battle.

A knight disgraced

The women viewed the banners and helms of the contestants before the tourney. If a lady knew that a knight had done wrong, his helmet was taken down and he was banned.

Devil take you

The church disliked tournaments because so much blood was often spilled. This 14th-century picture shows devils waiting to seize the souls of knights killed in a tourney.

Club tourney

In this type of tourney, two teams use blunt swords and clubs. Their crested helmets are fitted with face grilles. Each knight has a banner-bearer, while attendants stand ready in case he falls. The knight of honor rides between two ropes that separate the teams; ladies and judges are in the stands. Although the tournament grounds, or lists, had become smaller, the artist of this illustration has squashed them up to fit everything in.

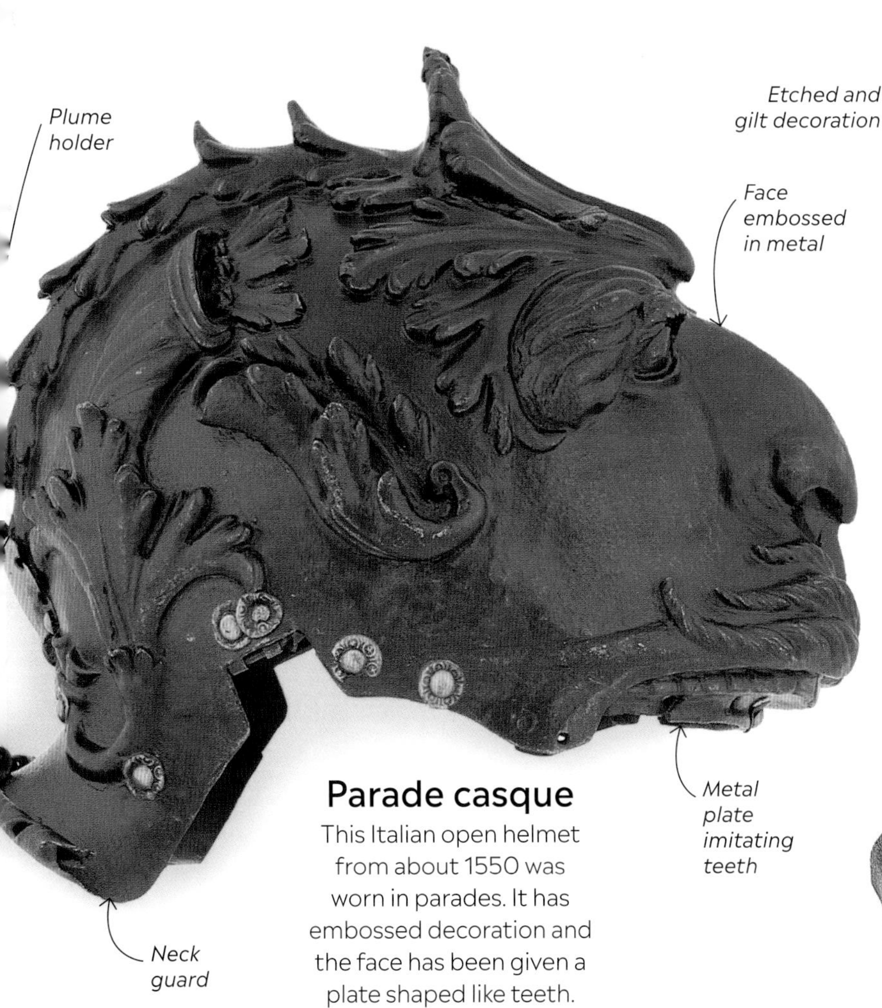

Parade casque

This Italian open helmet from about 1550 was worn in parades. It has embossed decoration and the face has been given a plate shaped like teeth. The hinged ear pieces are missing.

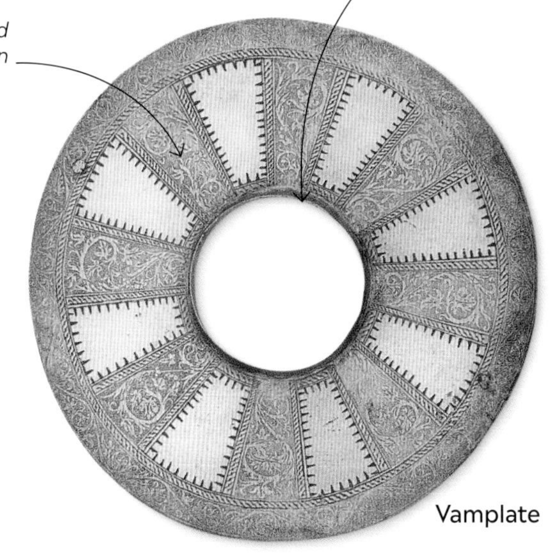

Vamplate

Vamplate and locking-gauntlet

The vamplate was fixed over the lance to guard the knight's hand. Once the knight had gripped his sword, the locking-gauntlet was locked shut so the sword was not lost in combat.

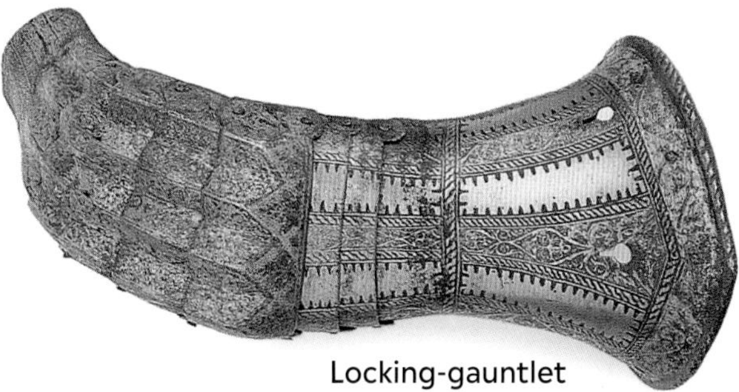

Locking-gauntlet

The joust

During the 13th century, jousts were added to tournaments. In this contest, two knights would charge toward one another at top speed and try to knock each other off their horse with a single blow of their lance. A knight could also score points if he broke his lance on his opponent's shield or helmet. Sometimes, sharp lances were used in combats called "jousts of war." Lances that were fitted with a blunt tip were used for combats known as "jousts of peace."

Frog-mouthed helm

This 15th-century helmet was used for jousts of peace. The wearer could see his opponent by leaning forward during the charge. He straightened up at the moment of impact, so that the "frog-mouthed" lower lip protected his eyes from the lance-head.

Lancer's shield

This German wooden shield from about 1485 is covered in leather and was probably used for the Rennen, a version of the jousts of war. The lance could be rested in the side recess.

Watery warriors

This 14th-century miniature shows that jousts could also take place on water. Two teams rowed toward one another while a man tried to knock his opponent off balance.

EYEWITNESS

Shane Adams

In 1997, Canadian equestrian athlete Shane Adams formed a jousting company called The Knights of Valor. He won the International Jousting Championships twice before forming the World Jousting Championship Association. Adams also hosted the TV game show "Full Metal Jousting."

Wooden lances

By the 16th century, wooden lances were made to splinter easily. Slightly thinner than those used for jousting, this 17th-century lance (left) was used to spear a ring hanging from a bracket.

Reinforcements

Knights took part in different types of combat, so armor was sometimes supplied with extra pieces to be made up in various ways. From southern Germany in 1550, the reinforcing pieces shown here are for a version of the jousts of peace known as the “tilt in the Italian fashion.” Extra protection is provided, mainly for the left side of the body, because the knights passed one another on that side. Knights did not need great maneuverability when jousting, so rigid extra pieces could be bolted on.

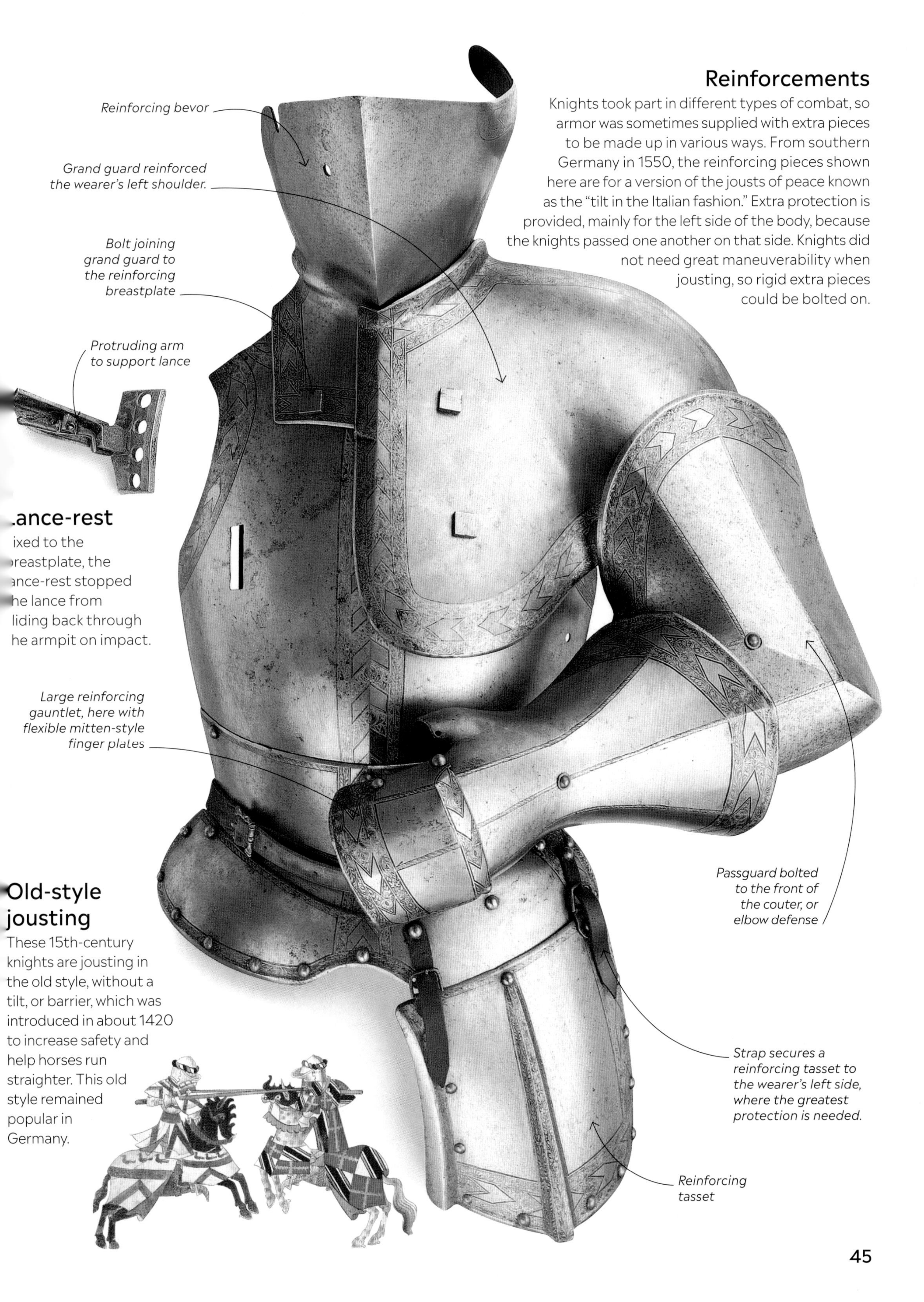

.ance-rest

ixed to the
ɔreastplate, the
ance-rest stopped
he lance from
liding back through
he armpit on impact.

Old-style jousting

These 15th-century knights are jousting in the old style, without a tilt, or barrier, which was introduced in about 1420 to increase safety and help horses run straighter. This old style remained popular in Germany.

Foot **combat**

In some 13th-century jousts, the knights dismounted and fought on with swords. By the 14th century, such foot combats were popular in their own right. Each knight was allowed a set number of blows, delivered alternately. From the 15th century, each man sometimes threw a javelin before fighting with a sword, ax, or staff weapon such as a poleax. Later, such combats were replaced by foot tournaments between two teams.

Formal fight

Foot combats in the 15th century took place without a barrier, so the contestants protected their legs with armor. The most common helmet for these contests was the great basinet seen below.

Brow reinforce

This plate was screwed to the visor of the helmet shown on the right.

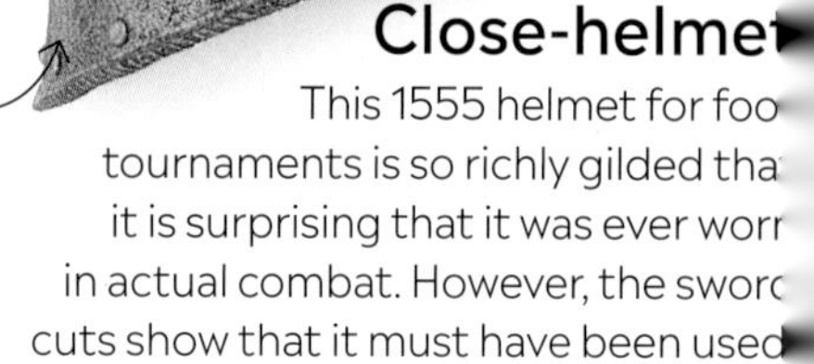

Close-helmet

This 1555 helmet for foo
tournaments is so richly gilded tha
it is surprising that it was ever worn
in actual combat. However, the sword
cuts show that it must have been used.

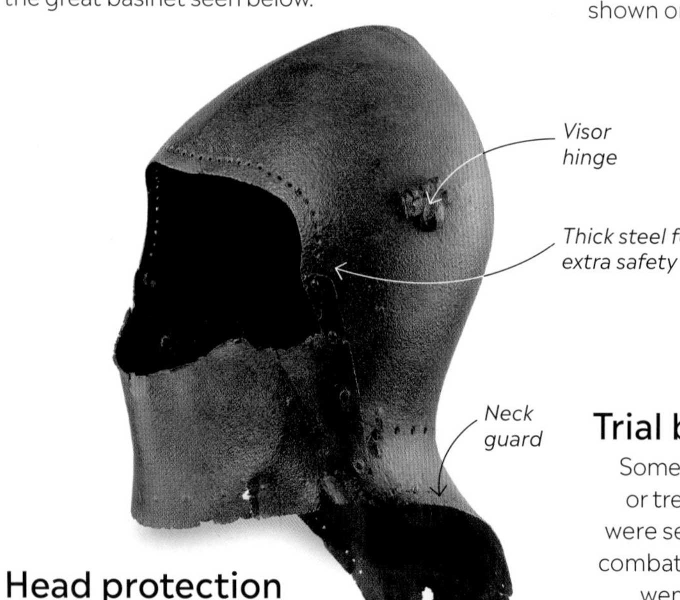

Head protection

Helmets, such as this 16th-century great basinet, had to be able to withstand direct blows at close quarters, so its steel might have been thicker than a battle helmet's.

Trial by battle

Sometimes murder or treason charges were settled by foot combat. The contest went on until the accused was either killed or surrendered, in which case he was executed. If he won he was judged innocent.

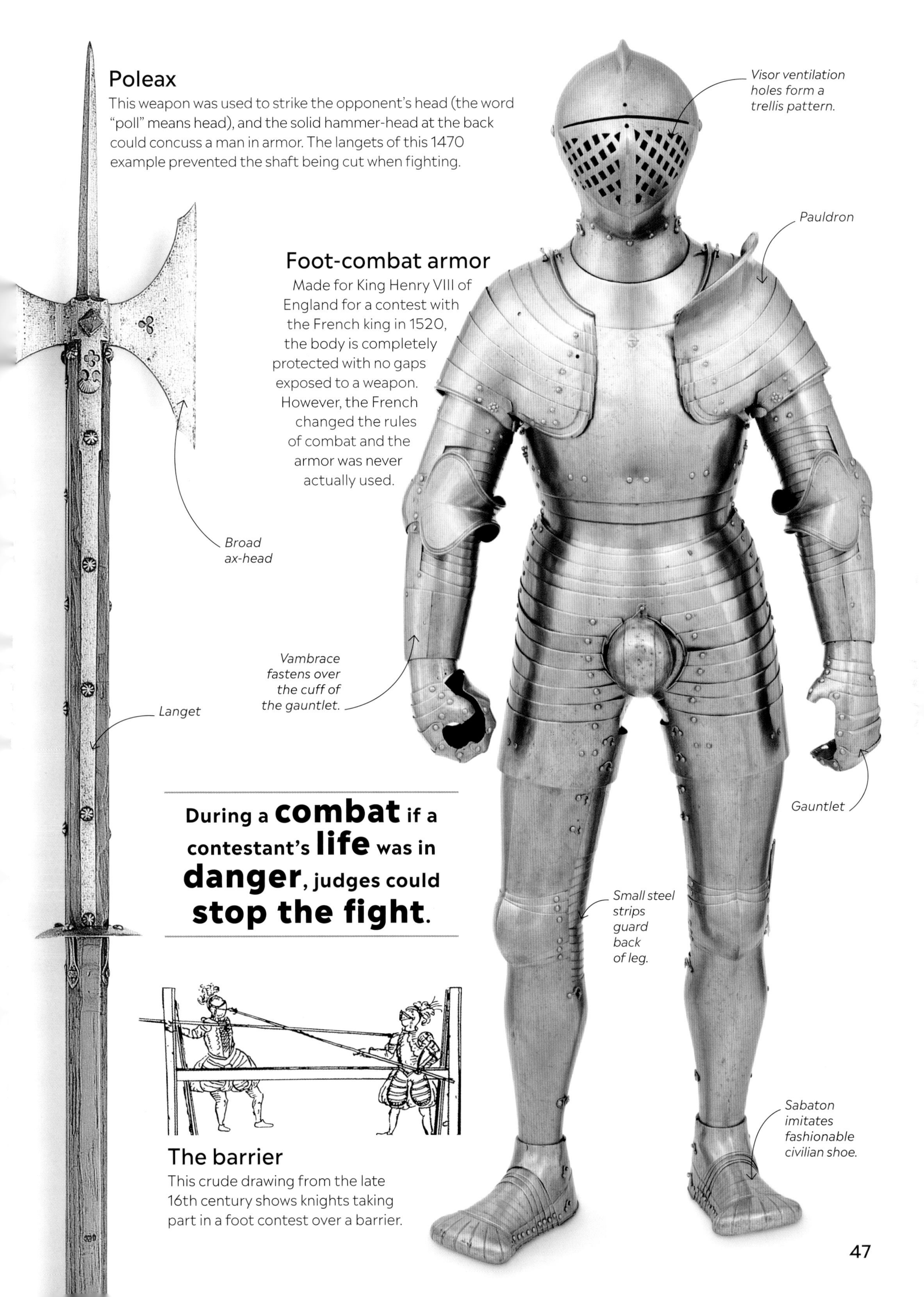
Visor ventilation holes form a trellis pattern.
Pauldron
Broad ax-head
Vambrace fastens over the cuff of the gauntlet.
Langet
Gauntlet
Small steel strips guard back of leg.
Sabaton imitates fashionable civilian shoe.

Poleax

This weapon was used to strike the opponent's head (the word "poll" means head), and the solid hammer-head at the back could concuss a man in armor. The langets of this 1470 example prevented the shaft being cut when fighting.

Foot-combat armor

Made for King Henry VIII of England for a contest with the French king in 1520, the body is completely protected with no gaps exposed to a weapon. However, the French changed the rules of combat and the armor was never actually used.

During a combat if a contestant's life was in danger, judges could stop the fight.

The barrier

This crude drawing from the late 16th century shows knights taking part in a foot contest over a barrier.

Heraldry

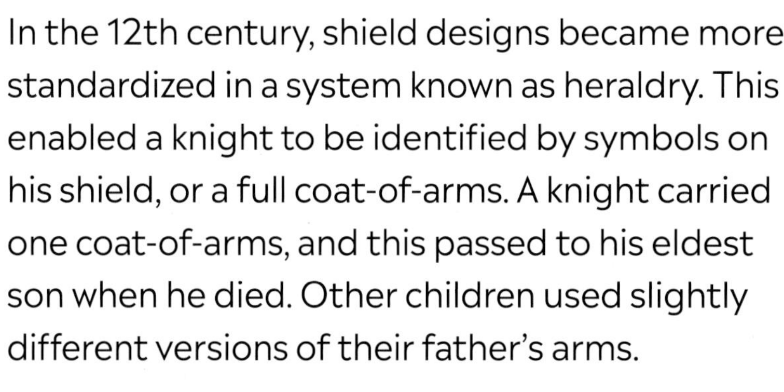

In the 12th century, shield designs became more standardized in a system known as heraldry. This enabled a knight to be identified by symbols on his shield, or a full coat-of-arms. A knight carried one coat-of-arms, and this passed to his eldest son when he died. Other children used slightly different versions of their father's arms.

Or, a pale gules

Azure, a fess embattled or

Sable, a cross engrailed or

Lozengy argent and gules

Vert, a crescent or

Azure, a fleur-de-lys or

Gules, a spur argent

Badge of office

This copper badge was worn by a servant of François de Lorraine, Hospitaller Prior of France from 1549 to 1563, whose arms it bears.

Majolica jar with coat-of-arms of a Portuguese nobleman

Heraldic jar

Coats-of-arms were also placed on objects. This jar, from about 1500, has quartered arms, in which the arms of two families joined by marriage appear twice together.

Costume design

A 16th-century picture shows James V of Scotland wearing a tabard with the royal arms. His wife, Mary of Guise, bears her French family arms.

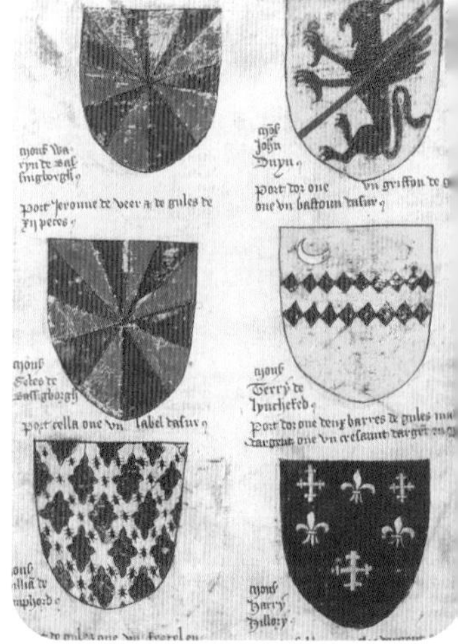

Roll of arms

The Carlisle Roll contains 276 shields of Edward III's personnel on his visit to Carlisle, England, in 1335.

A knight's shield

This rare surviving shield from the 13th century is made from wood, which has a lion rampant molded in leather. These are the arms of a ruler of Hesse, Germany.

Colorful spectacle

In this 15th-century picture, knights' shields hang over the sides of boats, largely for display. The French royal arms appear on trumpet banners and on a banner flying from a ship's masthead.

Arms of Cosimo de' Medici

word arms

tched with the rms of Cosimo e' Medici, Duke f Florence, this alian falchion, heavy-bladed utting sword, ates from the 6th century.

Pommel of gilt iron cast in shape of a lion's head

Making an impression

The bezel of this large 14th-century gold signet ring is engraved with heraldic arms of the de Grailly family. Above are the letters: "EID Gre," probably meaning: "This is the seal of Jean de Grailly."

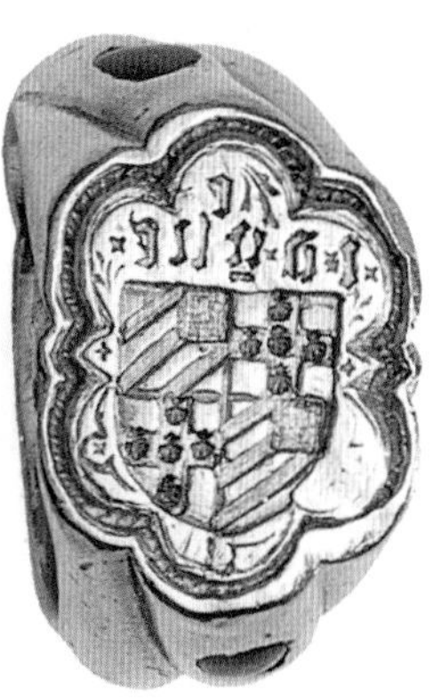

Gules, a lion rampant or

Or, a lion sejant regardant purpure

Gules, a swan argent

Azure, a dolphin naiant argent

Or, a dragon rampant vert

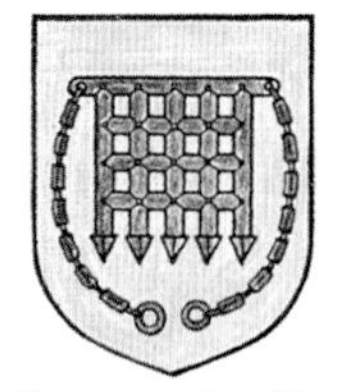

Or, a portcullis purpure

Azure, a sun in splendor or

KEY TO ARMS	
Or	Gold
Argent	Silver
Gules	Red
Azure	Blue
Sable	Black
Vert	Green
Purpure	Purple

A family affair

In this illustration from c. 1330, Sir Geoffrey Luttrell's heraldic arms are displayed on his surcoat, shoulder ailettes, shield, lance, horse's saddle, caparison, and head. They also appear on the dresses of his wife and daughter-in-law.

Coat-of-arms

This brass of Sir Thomas Blennerhassett (died 1531) shows the heraldic arms on his coat armor, the name given to the surcoat.

Hunting

Flying t a lu

A lure wa dummy bird th the falconer swu from a long co The falcon wou pounce on the lu so the falcon could retrie his bir

Medieval monarchs and lords were fond of hunting. The sport provided fresh meat, as well as helping to train knights for war. The Norman kings set aside vast areas of woodland for hunting in England. The animals hunted included deer, rabbits, boar, and birds. Sometimes, beaters drove the prey toward the huntsmen, who lay in wait. The peregrine falcon was considered one of the best hunting birds, because it was fast and agile, diving on its prey at incredible speed.

Noble beasts

This detail of the carving on the side of this crossbow tiller shows a stag hunt. Only rich people were allowed to hunt stags.

Steel pin to engage rack, a stee claw to win back the bowstring

Wooden tiller veneered with polished stag horn carved in relief

Wooden flights

Wooden feathers

Rather than feathers, these crossbow bolts from around 1470 have wooden flights.

Wolf hunt

Huntsmen used meat to lure wolves, who followed the scent. Lookouts in trees warned of the wolf's approach and mastiff dogs flushed it out. This hunt is from a 15th-century hunting book by Gaston Phoebus, Count of Foix, France.

For deer hunters

The blade of a 1540 German hunting sword, below, is etched with scenes of a stag hunt. Such swords were carried when hunting and were also used for general protection.

Deer being driven into nets

Dogs chasing the deer

Hunting horn

On the hunt

A Flemish or German silver plaque from around 1600 shows hunting with hounds, falconry, and shooting. One hound catches a hare in front of three ladies, who watch with interest from their carriage.

Weapon at the ready

The crossbow was a popular hunting weapon. It could be used on horseback and easily reloaded. The bowstring was drawn back (spanned) and hooked over a revolving nut until released by the trigger. This meant the crossbow could be ready in case any game was flushed out. Crossbows for use in hunting were sometimes lavishly decorated, as shown on this detailed 15th-century example.

Original bowstring of twisted cord

Bow bound to tiller by entwined cord and leather thongs

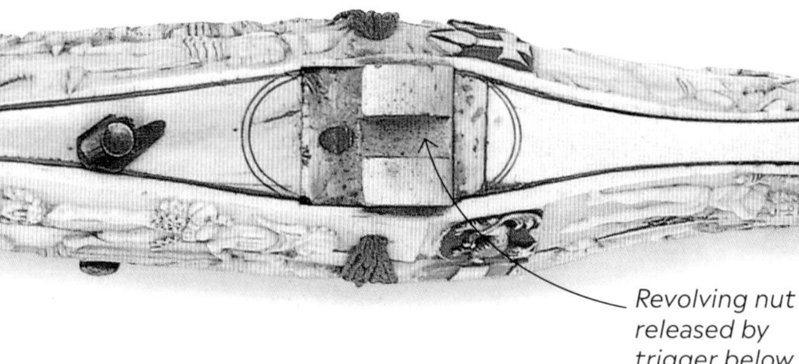

Triangular barbed head

Steel bow wrapped in gilded and painted parchment

Pet care

Hunting dogs needed to be looked after carefully, and Gaston Phoebus recommended using herbal medicines to cure diseases of the eye, ear, and throat. Broken legs were put in harnesses.

After them!

This 14th-century picture shows a lady blowing a hunting horn as she gallops after the dogs.

Boar-catcher

The boar spear was intended to stop an onrushing boar or even a bear. A cross-bar was provided to stop an enraged animal pushing up onto the shaft.

Faith and **pilgrimage**

The church played a major part in life in the Middle Ages. Western Europe was Roman Catholic until Protestantism took hold in some countries in the 16th century. Most people were religious and churches flourished, taking one-tenth of everyone's goods as a sort of tax. Some lords even became monks after a life of violence, hoping that this would make it easier for them to enter heaven.

Owner of the horn

This medallion shows Charles, Duke of Burgundy, who owned the Horn of St. Hubert.

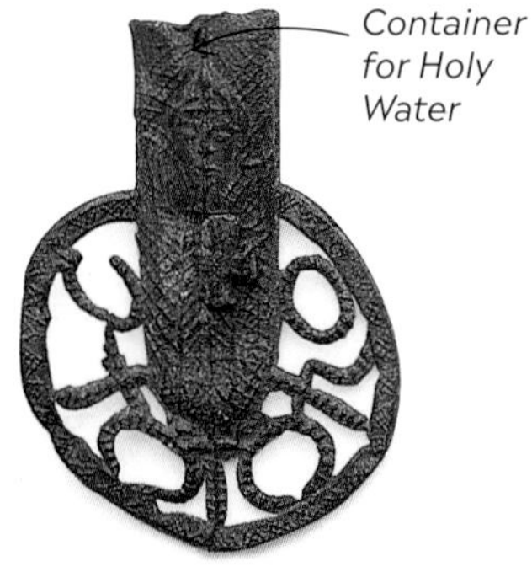

Water carrier

People wore tiny containers, called ampullae, holding holy water to protect them from evil. This one has a picture of St. Thomas Becket, killed at Canterbury, England, in 1170.

Knight at prayer

The saints played a vital part in people's lives. This stained-glass window shows a knight praying at a statue of Mary Magdalene.

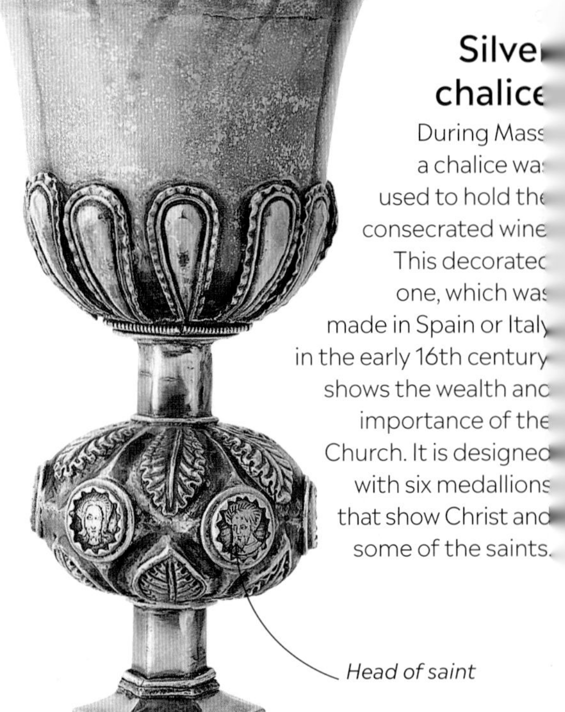

Silve chalice

During Mass a chalice wa used to hold th consecrated wine This decorate one, which wa made in Spain or Ital in the early 16th century shows the wealth an importance of the Church. It is designed with six medallion that show Christ and some of the saints.

Lead pilgrim badge of St. Catherine

Symbols of faith

People wore badges, such as this lead cross, to show that they had been on a pilgrimage. Other symbols included Christ and the Virgin Mary, and the saints.

Lead seal showing the Virgin Mary holding the baby Jesus

[H]orn of St. Hubert

[M]edieval people liked to touch or even [p]ossess relics of the dead saints, even [th]ough some had no connection with the [re]al saint. St. Hubert was said to have seen [th]e vision of a cross shining between a [d]eer's antlers, and he became the patron [s]aint of huntsmen.

To be a pilgrim

These 13th-century pilgrims are traveling to the Holy Land [o]f Jerusalem, but getting there meant a long and dangerous journey. Pilgrims to Jerusalem wore a palm-leaf badge.

Missionary

The Church was always eager to convert others to Christianity, either through teaching or by more forceful methods. Here, Friar Odoric receives a blessing before he goes to the East as a missionary. Knights might also seek blessings before dangerous journeys.

The Canterbury Tales

Between 1387 and 1400, Geoffrey Chaucer (right) wrote *The Canterbury Tales*, which is about a pilgrimage. One tale sees a knight (left) and his son tell stories along the way to pass the time.

Chaucer's knight

Geoffrey Chaucer

Processional cross

This early-15th-century Italian silver cross has been partly gilded and decorated with enamels. The Virgin Mary, St. John, and St. Nicholas are shown on the arms of the cross. The pelican is a symbol of piety—people thought that she wounded herself in order to feed her young, a symbol of Christ bleeding for all sinners.

The crusades

In 1095 at Clermont, France, Pope Urban II launched a militar expedition to capture the Christian holy places in Jerusalen from the Muslim Turks ruling the Holy Land: this became know as the First Crusade. The crusaders captured Jerusalem in 109 and established the Kingdom of Jerusalem. However, the cit was lost again in 1187 and all later crusades failed. Crusade were also led against the Moors in Spain, pagan Slavs i northeastern Europe, and non-Catholic Christians

People's crusade

In 1096, French preacher Peter the Hermit led a mob from Cologne, Germany, toward Jerusalem. They were wiped out in Anatolia (modern Türkiye) by the Turks.

Spanish crusaders

In Spain, from the 11th century, Christian armies fought the Muslims until their last stronghold fell in 1492. Warrior monks, such as the Order of Santiago seen here, helped the Christian reconquest of Spain.

King on a tile

These decorated tiles from Chertsey Abbey, England, show Richard the Lionheart a leader of the Third Crusade (1189–1192). Richard realized that even if he recaptured Jerusalem, the Christians could not hold it after he left.

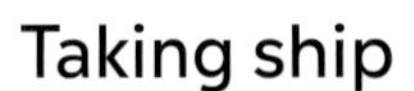

Taking ship

There were two routes from Europe to the Holy Land: the dangerous road overland or across the Mediterranean Sea. The Italian city-states of Venice, Pisa, and Genoa, eager for new trade, often provided ships to crusader forces.

This 14th-century manuscript shows crusaders preparing to sail for the Holy Land.

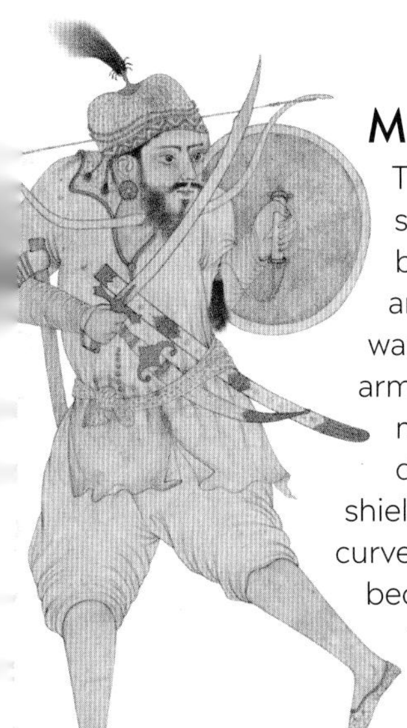

Muslim warrior

This Turkish foot soldier carries a bow, sabre, dagger and axe. Some warriors wore plate armor, but many wore mail or padded defenses. Round shields were common; curved, slashing sabers became popular in the 12th century.

Fighting for the faith

This picture shows Christians and Muslims clashing in 1218 during the Christian siege of Damietta, Egypt.

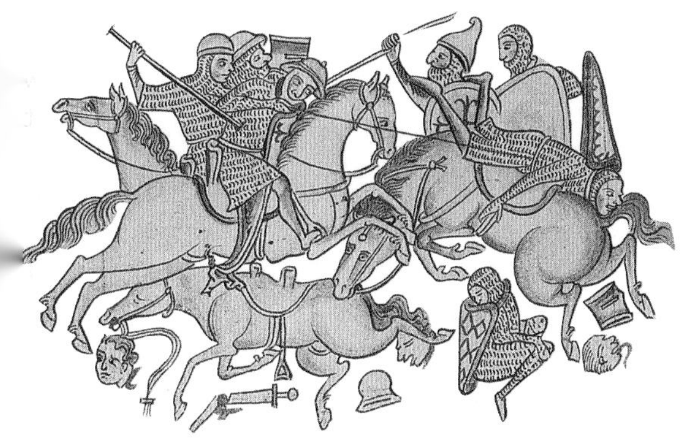

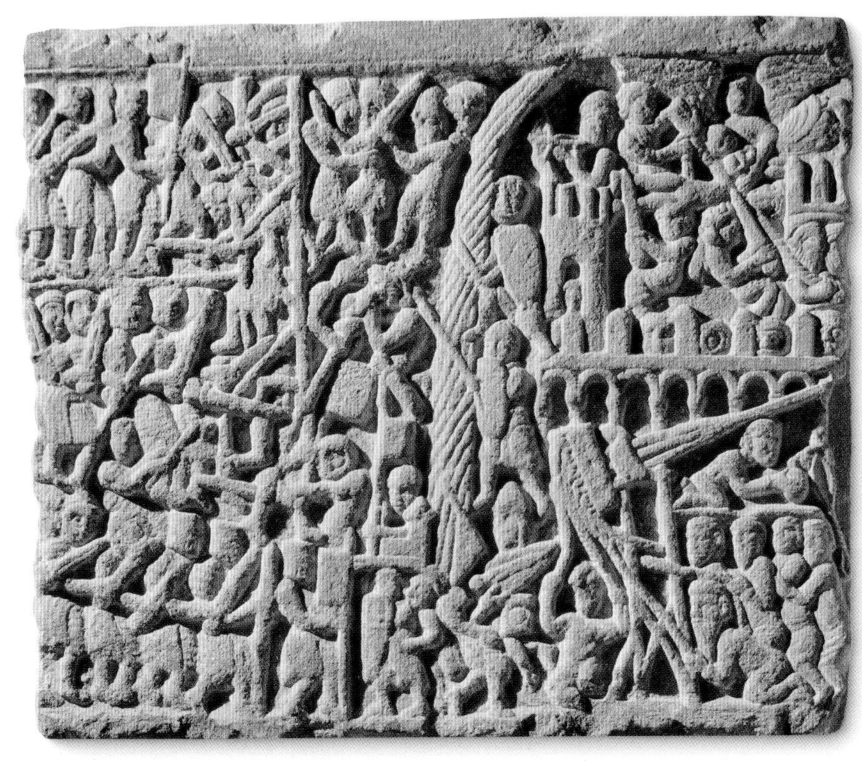

Albigensian Crusade

In 1209, the Albigensian Crusade was called for by the Pope against the Cathars, a Christian group who did not accept the teachings of the Roman Catholic Church. This stone carving shows men hauling on the ropes of a trebuchet at the siege of Carcassonne in Southern France during the crusade.

The Mamluks

Mamluks, a group of Muslim slave soldiers, ruled Egypt and Syria in 1250–1517. They fought the crusaders, capturing the Levant (eastern Mediterranean) in 1302. Muslims rode fast, nimble mounts, unlike the slower, sturdier crusader horses. Despite differences in culture and beliefs, Christian and Muslim warriors shared elements of knighthood in common.

An Egyptian plaque of c. 1330 shows a Mamluk warrior shooting arrows from horseback.

EYEWITNESS

Saladin

Kurdish military leader Saladin (c. 1137–1193) managed to unite the Muslim tribes of the Holy Land. He defeated the king of Jerusalem's army and recaptured the city in 1187. Saladin was respected as a chivalrous leader even by his European opponents.

Knights of **Christ**

In 1118, a band of knights protecting Christian pilgrims in the Holy Land formed a religious order, although they continued to fight the Muslims. This order was known as the Knights Templar. In the same period, an order of monks who treated the sick became a military order called the Knights of St. John, or Knights Hospitaller. After the Christians lost control of the Holy Land in 1291, the Hospitallers moved to the Mediterranean and continued fighting. The German Teutonic Order of Knights was formed in 1198.

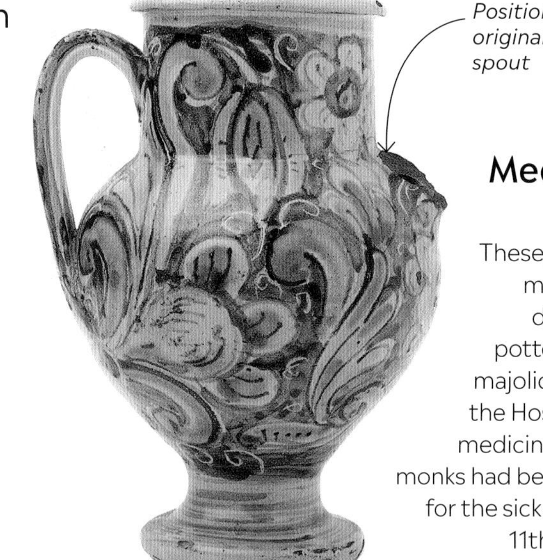

Medicin ja

These jars wer made fror decorate pottery calle majolica to hol the Hospitallers medicines. These monks had been carinc for the sick since the 11th century

The fight goes on

After the loss of the Holy Land, the Hospitallers moved, first to Cyprus, then to Rhodes in 1310, where they again clashed with the Muslims.

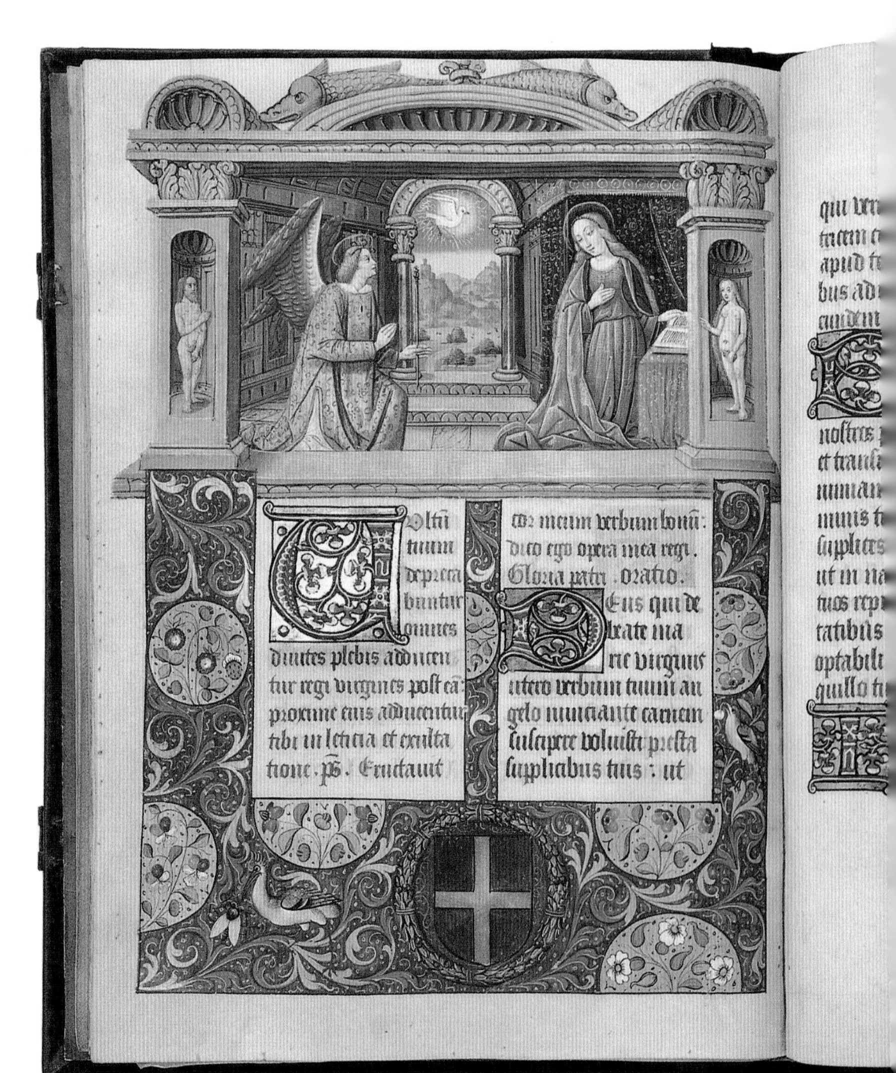

EYEWITNESS

St. Ubaldesca

Between the 12th and 13th centuries, many women joined Hospitaller orders. Ubaldesca (c. 1136–1205) joined the House of Giovanni in Pisa (in what is now Italy) when she was 14 and worked for the nuns there for the next 55 years. She was declared a saint around 60 years after her death.

Templars burning

After the Holy Land had been lost to the Muslims, the French king sought to ize the wealth the Templars nad amassed. He executed neir Grand Master, Jacques de Molay, and in 1314, suppressed the order.

The hospital

Malta was the final home of the Hospitallers. This 1586 engraving shows them in the great ward of their hospital in the Maltese capital, Valletta.

Grand Master's seal

This seal belonged to Raymond de Bérenger, who ran the Hospitallers from 1365 to 1374.

Processional cross

This early-16th-century cross is made of oak covered with silver plate; the figure of Christ is older. The Evangelists are pictured on the arms of the cross, which belonged to the Hospitallers. The coat of arms is that of Pierre Decluys, Grand Prior of France from 1522 to 1535.

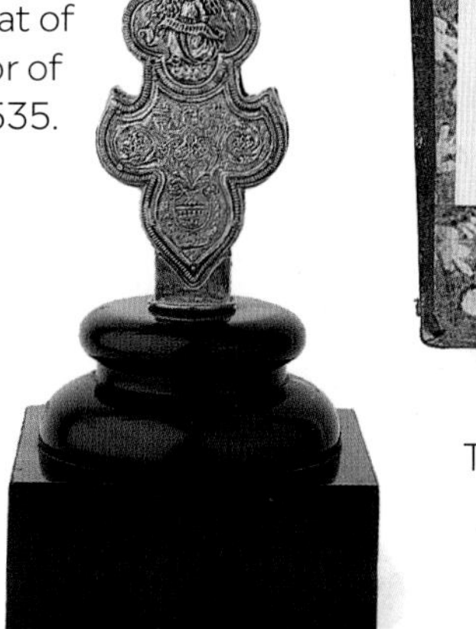

Order of service

The Knights of St. John were expected to attend church and to know their Bible. Breviaries, like the one above, contained the daily service. The religious knights had to obey strict rules, which were usually based on those of the regular monastic orders.

Knight Templar

Templars wore a white surcoat with a red cross. This 12th-century fresco from a Templar church in France shows a knight galloping into battle.

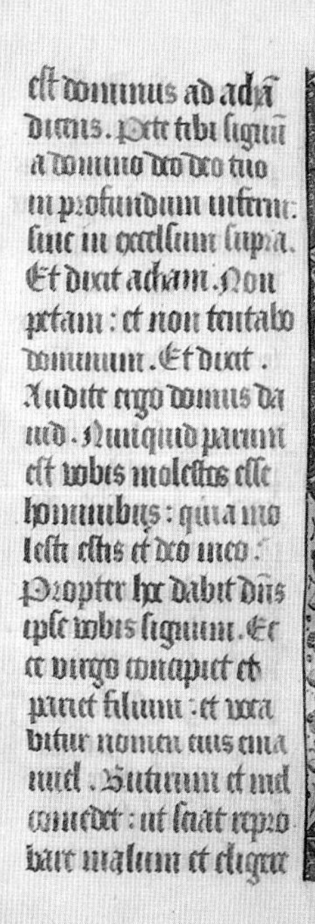

est dominus ad achā
dicens. Pete tibi signū
a domino deo tuo
in profundum inferni:
sive in excelsum supra.
Et dixit achaz. Non
petam: et non temptabo
dominum. Et dixit.
Audite ergo domus da
uid. Numquid parum
est vobis molestos esse
hominibus: quia mo
lesti estis et deo meo?
Propter hoc dabit dns
ipse vobis signum. Ec
ce virgo concipiet et
pariet filium: et voca
bitur nomen eius ema
nuel. Butirum et mel
comedet: ut sciat repro
bare malum et eligere

The Rhodes Missal

The Knights Hospitaller swore to serve the order faithfully, never marry, and help those in need. It is thought that many knights took their vows on this book, the late-15th-century Rhodes Missal.

Teutonic Knights

The Teutonic Knights also fought tribes in eastern Europe to force them to become Roman Catholic. The 13th-century German knightly poet Tannhäuser (left) is wearing the cloak of the Teutonic Order.

Japanese **knights**

Japan developed a society similar to medieval Europe, and the equivalent of the knight was the samurai. After the Gempei War of 1180–1185, Japan was ruled by an emperor, but real power lay with the military leader, or shogun. Later, civil war weakened the shogun's authority, but a strong shogunate was revived after a victory in 1600, and the last great samurai battle was fought in 1615.

Helmet and face guar

Helmets like this 17th-century examp have a neck guard made of iron plat coated with lacquer (a type of varnis and were laced together with si

Early armor

Worn by mounted archers, this 19th-century copy of 12th-century armor (above) is in the great armor, or *Ō-yoroi*, style. The cuirass is made of small, lacquered iron plates.

Fighting samurai

From the 14th century, an increase in foot combat meant the nobility abandoned the *Ō-yoroi* armor for other styles. Similar to "knight," samurai means "those who closely serve the nobility."

Swordsman

Samurai prized their swords greatly. In this 19th-century print, a samurai is about to strike with his sword, before his opponent can unsheathe the *tachi* (long sword) hanging at his side.

Wakizashi

Tempered edge

Katana

Pair of swords

The main samurai sword was the *katana*, sheathed in a wooden scabbard (*saya*), with a rough sharkskin grip (*tsuka*). The pair of swords (*daisho*) was completed by a shorter sword (*wakizashi*).

Master and servant

This small lacquered case, or *inro*, depicts a servant kneeling before a samurai. Samurai needed servants to attend them and to care for their equipment. A samurai held life-and-death power over his servants and over the farmers who worked on his land and provided him with food.

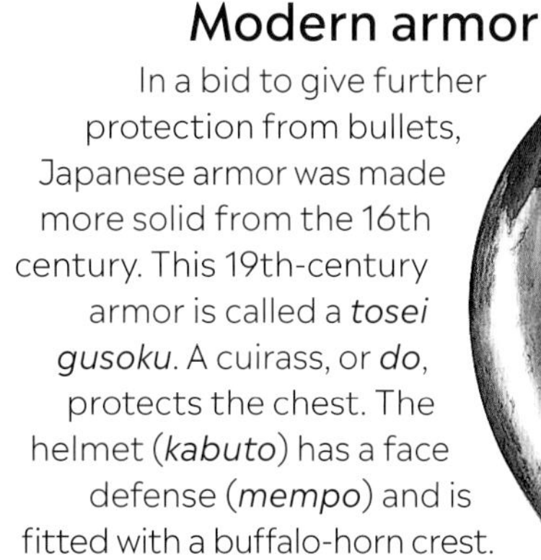

Modern armor

In a bid to give further protection from bullets, Japanese armor was made more solid from the 16th century. This 19th-century armor is called a *tosei gusoku*. A cuirass, or *do*, protects the chest. The helmet (*kabuto*) has a face defense (*mempo*) and is fitted with a buffalo-horn crest.

Swordsmanship

In this 19th-century picture, a samurai is instructed in swordplay by creatures called *tengu*. Learning to use the sword correctly took years of hard work.

Sharkskin grip

Metal plates (kusazuri) protect the hips and upper thighs.

EYEWITNESS

Hangaku Gozen

Women in Japan could not become samurai or fight battles. But there were exceptions. Hangaku Gozen was a member of the Taira clan and took part in the Kennin Rebellion against the shogun in 1201. Defending Torisaka Castle, in present-day Shikoku, she shot down enemies with arrows.

The **professionals**

Over time, feudal forces who fought in return for their land were replaced by permanent forces of well-trained, paid soldiers. Mounted knights were also becoming less effective on the battlefield. Heavily armed squadrons of knights could not break the disciplined ranks of infantry. By 1500, the infantry was becoming the most important part of any army.

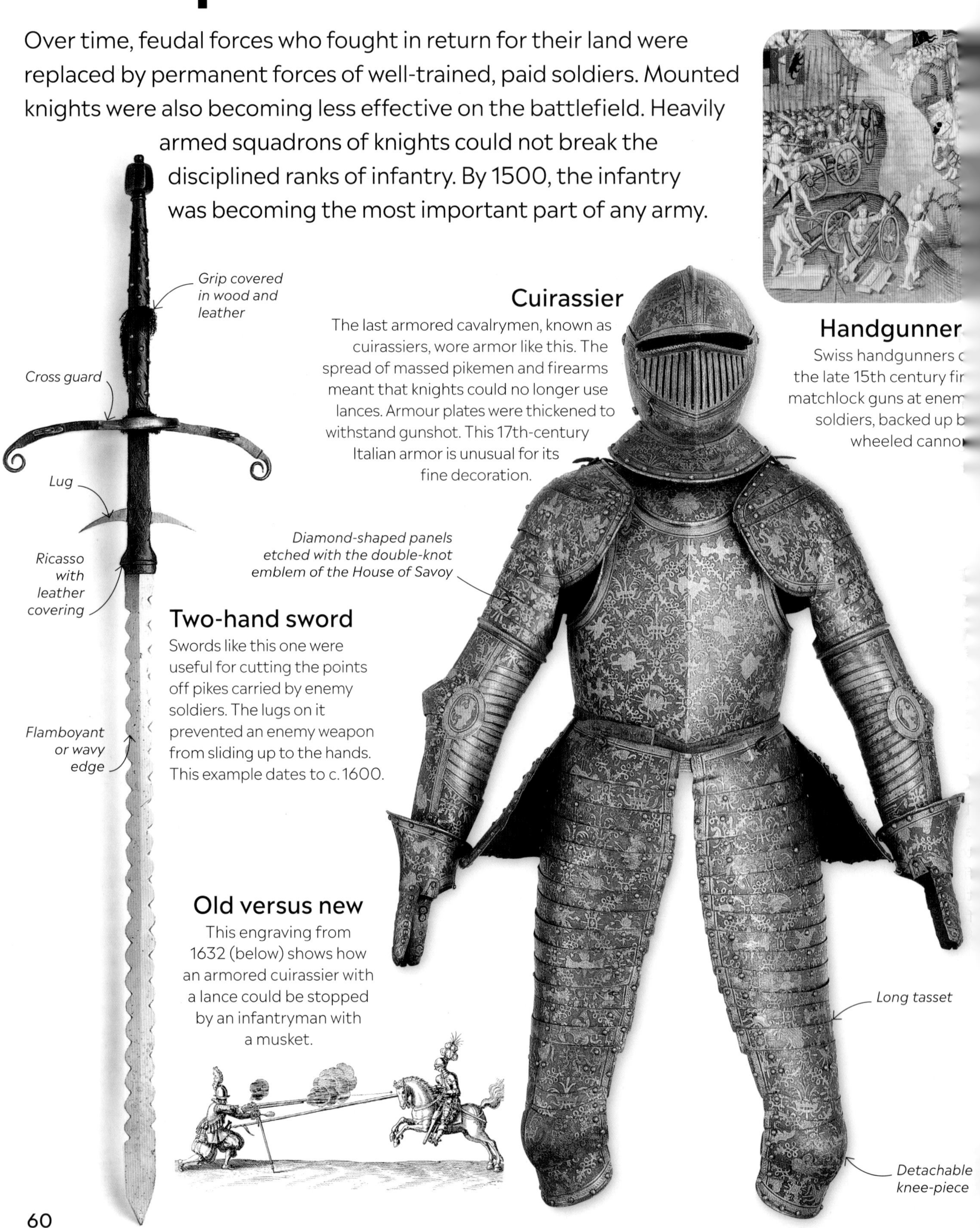

Handgunner

Swiss handgunners c
the late 15th century fir
matchlock guns at enem
soldiers, backed up b
wheeled canno

Cuirassier

The last armored cavalrymen, known as cuirassiers, wore armor like this. The spread of massed pikemen and firearms meant that knights could no longer use lances. Armour plates were thickened to withstand gunshot. This 17th-century Italian armor is unusual for its fine decoration.

Two-hand sword

Swords like this one were useful for cutting the points off pikes carried by enemy soldiers. The lugs on it prevented an enemy weapon from sliding up to the hands. This example dates to c. 1600.

Old versus new

This engraving from 1632 (below) shows how an armored cuirassier with a lance could be stopped by an infantryman with a musket.

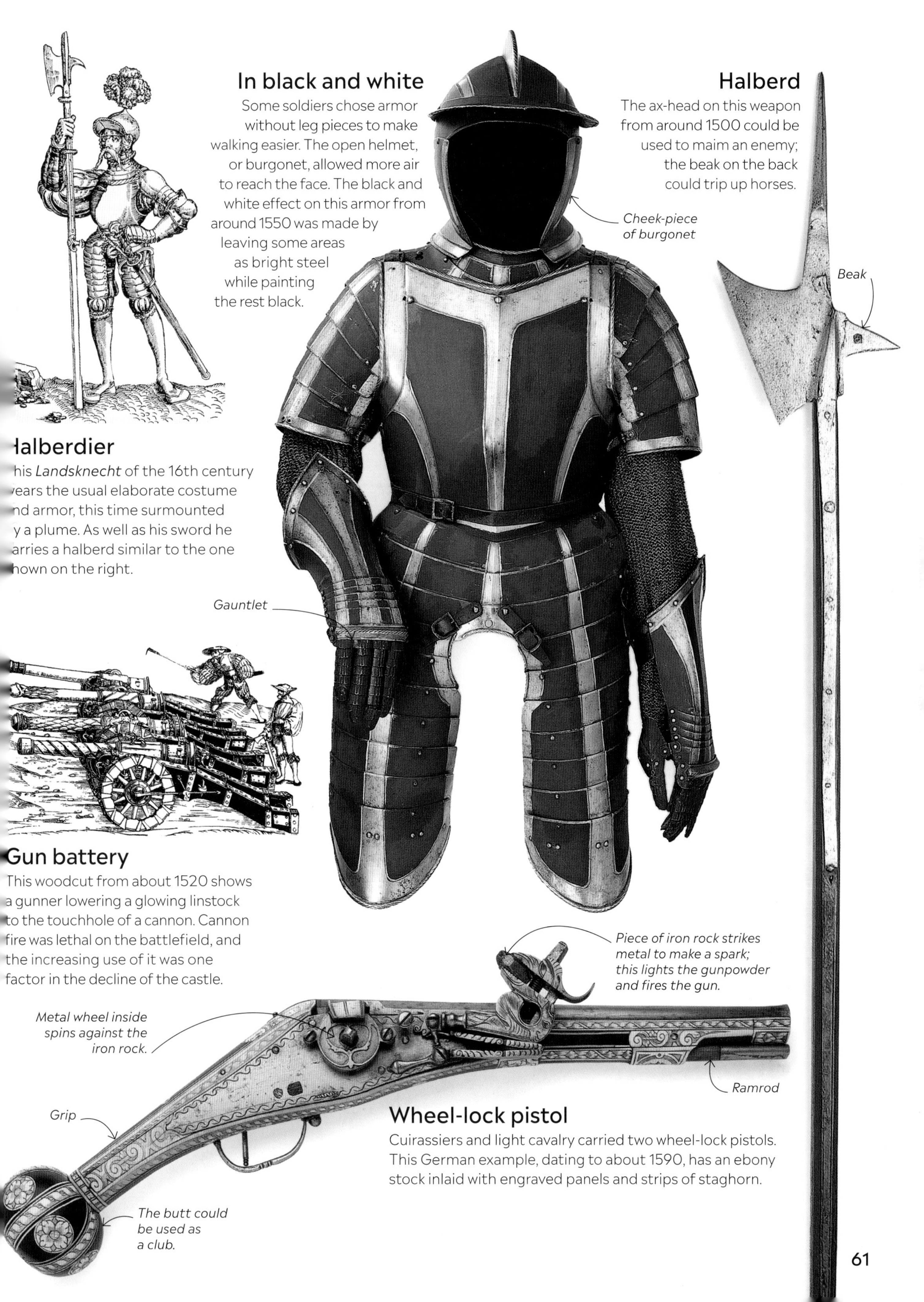
Cheek-piece
of burgonet
Beak
Gauntlet
Piece of iron rock strikes
metal to make a spark;
this lights the gunpowder
and fires the gun.
Metal wheel inside
spins against the
iron rock.
Ramrod
Grip
The butt could
be used as
a club.

In black and white

Some soldiers chose armor without leg pieces to make walking easier. The open helmet, or burgonet, allowed more air to reach the face. The black and white effect on this armor from around 1550 was made by leaving some areas as bright steel while painting the rest black.

Halberd

The ax-head on this weapon from around 1500 could be used to maim an enemy; the beak on the back could trip up horses.

Halberdier

This *Landsknecht* of the 16th century wears the usual elaborate costume and armor, this time surmounted by a plume. As well as his sword he carries a halberd similar to the one shown on the right.

Gun battery

This woodcut from about 1520 shows a gunner lowering a glowing linstock to the touchhole of a cannon. Cannon fire was lethal on the battlefield, and the increasing use of it was one factor in the decline of the castle.

Wheel-lock pistol

Cuirassiers and light cavalry carried two wheel-lock pistols. This German example, dating to about 1590, has an ebony stock inlaid with engraved panels and strips of staghorn.

Knights' end

By the 17th century, warfare was becomin
more the job of full-time soldiers, althoug
knights might have still fought as officers
Knighthood increasingly became a titl
given to people the monarch though
deserved recognition. But the image of th
medieval knight was not forgotten. During
the 19th century there was renewed interest
seen in art, architecture, and books, while in the
20th century, film and television brough
knights to the screen

Herald's tabard

This tabard was worn by a herald of Queen Anne (reigned 1702–1714) and bears the arms of England, Scotland, Ireland, and France. Heralds continue to grant new coats-of-arms, maintain registers, and give advice on planning ceremonial events.

Modern reenactment

In the late 20th century, reenactment of knightly battles and jousts became popular. This led to an increased demand for authentic costume and armor, providing work for specialized craftspeople. Many enthusiasts re-create historical events, such as the Battle of Grunwald shown here.

St. George slaying a dragon

Smithsonian Castle

Castles remained as romantic ruins, inspiring poets and writers. Those with enough wealth even built their own versions, such as this one in Washington, D.C., completed in 1855 as a museum for the Smithsonian Institution.

Order of the Garter

Created in 1348, the Garter is the oldest order of English knighthood. It is the highest award the monarch can give a person for their achievements. This Lesser George badge, one of the order's insignias, dates from between 1800 and 1850.

Investiture ceremony

In 1969, Prince Charles (now King Charles III) was made Prince of Wales by his mother, Queen Elizabeth II, in Caernarfon Castle, Wales. This echoed the first-ever investiture of a Prince of Wales, in 1301.

Did you **know?**

AMAZING FACTS

The expression "to get on your high horse" means to be overbearing or arrogant. It comes from the Middle Ages, when people of high rank rode on taller horses than those of lower rank.

Knight riding high on horseback

During a siege, a trebuchet was sometimes used to throw very unpleasant missiles into a castle, including severed heads, dead animals, and cattle dung.

Spiral staircases in medieval castles made life difficult for an attacker fighting his way up, because his weapon (in his right hand) would keep hitting the post in the center of the stairs.

Due to the damp climate in Japan, samurai armor had to be lacquered to stop it rusting.

Pivoting wooden arm

Sling pouch

Trebuchet

Krak des Chevalie

The badge of the Knights Templar Order was two knights riding on one horse. This represented their original state of poverty.

The name Templars came from their headquarters' location, which was situated near the old Jewish temple in Jerusalem.

King Richard I, known as Richard the Lionheart, ruled England from 1189 to 1199. He was a heroic fighter and zealous crusader, and was committed to the ideal of chivalry.

The castle of Krak des Chevaliers in Syria was a crusader castle built in the 12th century. The Knights Hospitaller lived there. The castle was damaged between 2012 and 2013 during the Syrian Civil War.

Medieval pilgrims wore badges on their hats to show they had been to a shrine.

In 1212, about 30,000 French and German children took part in a crusade to the Holy Land. Many of them never returned home. It was called the Children's Crusade.

Castle defenders often dropped missiles onto attackers below. Hot water, red-hot sand, rocks, or quicklime were also used.

The siege of Jerusalem by the Christian crusaders in 1099

UESTIONS AND ANSWERS

hat does chivalry mean?

ring the Middle Ages the word "chivalry" ferred to the knightly class. It comes om the French word for horse. But in ne chivalry came to mean the qualities pected of an ideal knight, such as urtesy, bravery, and honor.

ere tournaments dangerous?

tournament, or tourney, was a mock battle, it it could be very dangerous and bloody. one tourney, held in Neuss, Germany, more ian 60 knights were killed.

hat happened to knights who ere defeated in battle?

a knight defeated an opponent, he would ot always kill him. An enemy knight could be nore valuable alive than dead, if his family ould pay ransom money to get him back.

o knights still exist today?

nights in shining armor only exist in nuseums, but knighthood still remains in ritain, France, and Italy. In Britain, different rders of knighthood can be given by the nonarch to a British subject for outstanding ervice to the country.

Who built the first English castle?

t is hard to know for sure, but when William of Normandy invaded England in 1066, his soldiers placed fortifications in the old Roman fort at Pevensey. They then may have built a motte and bailey at Hastings, and waited for the arrival of King Harold and his army.

Scene from a medieval tournament

What were the crusades to the Holy Land?

The crusades (1095–1270) were a series of holy wars launched by Christian leaders to try and take over the Holy Land (the region in the Middle East sacred to Jews, Muslims, and Christians).

RECORD BREAKERS

Longest ride in armor
The longest recorded ride in armor was 208 miles (335 km) by Dick Brown. He left Edinburgh on June 10, 1989, and arrived in Dumfries four days later. The total riding time was 35 hours 25 minutes.

The most knights
During the reign of Henry II (1154–1189), the king could call upon the services of more than 6,000 knights. Each knight pledged to serve in his army for 40 days each year without pay.

The most expensive king
When Richard I of England was captured by the Duke of Austria in 1192, England paid a ransom of 150,000 marks. This sum is equivalent to many millions of dollars today.

Soldiers constructing what could be the first English castle, in 1066

Timeline

In 10th-century Europe, knights fought for their lords. Knightly honor, or chivalry, was born in the 12th century. By the 16th century, armies using pikes and guns replaced the armored knight. Knights also lived in Japan, and had an impact in other countries too.

768-814 Charlemagne employs mounted warriors Charlemagne, leader of the Franks, and his warriors conquer much of present-day France, Germany, the Low Countries, and Italy.

800 Charlemagne is crowned Emperor On Christmas Day 800, Charlemagne is crowned Emperor of the West by the Pope in Rome. This new empire lasts for more than 1,000 years.

814 Charlemagne dies After the death of Charlemagne, his empire breaks up. Local lords, and those mounted warrior knights who serve them, offer protection to local people in return for labor, giving rise to the feudal system in Europe.

c. 850 First castles built Earth and timber castles are built in France to protect the local lord. Castles are also built of stone about a century later.

900s The new order of knights A new social order of mounted, armored knights develops in parts of western Europe. They serve a local lord, duke, or king, and are in turn served by serfs or peasants.

911 Normandy founded Charles III of France gives land to Viking invaders in an attempt to stop them invading his country. The land is called Normandy, "land of the Northmen."

1000s Becoming a squire At first, many squires are from lower social classes. Boys of noble birth also train as squires, as part of their path to becoming knights.

1066 Normans invade England Duke William of Normandy invades England and defeats King Harold at the Battle of Hastings. William introduces the feudal system and builds castles made of timber and increasingly of stone.

1095 The crusades begin The Pope launches the first crusade against the Muslim occupation of the Holy Land. Many knights join this army. Further crusades are launched from Europe until Acre, the last Christian stronghold in the Holy Land, is captured by a Muslim army in 1291.

1118 Knights Templar formed in Jerusalem Knights protecting Christian pilgrims in the Holy Land form a religious military order known as the Knights Templar.

1100s Added protection Knights start to add more mail to their armor to protect their arms and legs.

1100s The code of chivalry A code of conduct, known as chivalry, is adopted by all knights. It requires them to behave in a courteous and civil way when dealing with their enemies and places special emphasis on courtly manners toward women.

1100s The first tournaments Tournaments, or mock battles, are first fought to train knights for battle. These events take place over a large stretch of countryside.

1100s The birth of heraldry Decorations on shields now become more standardized using a set of rules known as heraldry. This increasingly elaborate system enables a knight to be identified by the symbols on his shield, or by his full coat-of-arms.

1100s New siege machines The first trebuchets—pivoting sling catapults—are used in siege warfare in western rope. They join existing weapons, ch as catapults, battering rams, and llistas (large, mounted crossbows) besieging and attacking castles.

00s Age of the troubadours oubadours, or minstrels, from uthern France popularize poems courtly love, romance, and chivalry. ories about King Arthur and his ights of the round table become creasingly popular throughout estern Europe.

185 Shogun, Japan A samurai warrior ass led by the shogun, or military ader, takes power in Japan, although he emperor is still the official ruler f the country.

189-1199 Richard I Richard Coeur de ion, nicknamed "the Lionheart," rules ngland. He fights in the third crusade, rom 1190 to 1192, and is a prisoner from 192 to 1194.

198 The Teutonic Knights This new eligious and military order of knights s formed to fight in the crusades, but oon focuses on converting pagans o Christianity in eastern Europe.

1200s Added horsepower Most knights have two warhorses, as well as a destrier for jousting, a sumpter, or packhorse, for carrying baggage, and a palfrey for arduous long journeys.

1200s Safer tournaments Blunted weapons are introduced to make the tournaments safer. A new form of contest—jousts—is also introduced, in which two knights fight on horseback with lances or sometimes swords.

1200s The rising cost of knighthood The cost of becoming a knight is so expensive that many young men avoid being knighted and remain as squires.

1250s New plate armor Gradually, knights begin adding plates to their armor to protect the body further. The coat-of-plates first appears, made of pieces of metal riveted to a cloth.

1270s New weapons Along with the armor plates that knights increasingly wear, longer and heavier cutting swords appear, together with pointed swords that can be thrust between the plates.

1300s The arrival of cannons Cannons now appear on the battlefield to replace battering rams, catapults, and other manual machines for sieges.

1300s Foot combat Combat between two knights on foot becomes popular at tournaments. The knights use swords and are allowed a set number of blows. By the 1400s, such contests have developed into more complex events involving javelins and axes as well as swords.

1300s Defense against the knight In 1302, Flemish foot soldiers using clubs defeat French mounted knights at the Battle of Courtrai. In 1314, Scottish spear formations using pikes stop a charge by English mounted knights and defeat them at the Battle of Bannockburn. Both battles prove that knights are not invincible.

1337-1453 The Hundred Years' War In 1337, Edward III of England claims the French throne and invades the country. War between the two countries continues on and off for more than 100 years. Thanks to their longbowmen, the English achieve victories over French knights at Crécy (1346), Poitiers (1356), and Agincourt (1415).

1400 Full body armor Knights begin to wear full suits of plate armor, giving them all-over body protection.

1419-c. 1434 The Hussite Wars After Jan Hus was executed for heresy, his followers in Bohemia go to war with Catholic loyalists, using early firearms and cannon in wagon fortresses.

1476-1477 Swiss Confederation v. Burgundy War between the Swiss Confederation and Burgundy shows how mounted knights are unable to defeat solid bodies of pikemen backed up by soldiers using handguns.

1494 France invades Italy France's invasion of Italy in 1494 leads to a long power struggle in Europe between France and the Hapsburg empire of Spain and Austria.

1500s Designer armor Knights still wearing armor etch designs into the metal with acid; gold plating is sometimes used.

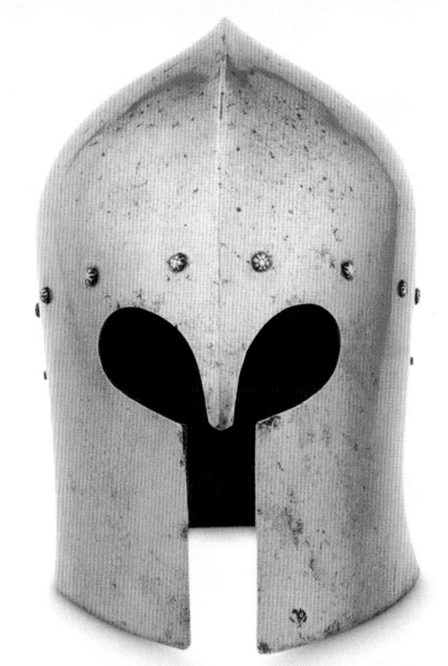

Italian barbute or iron helmet, 1445

1500s A professional army Paid armies of well-trained soldiers, backed up by mercenaries and locally recruited men, gradually replace the feudal armies of previous years. Knights now play a less effective role in battle.

1517 The Reformation In Germany Martin Luther starts a revolt against the Roman Catholic Church that leads to the creation of Protestant churches throughout western Europe.

1600s The end of the tournament During the 1600s, the tournament is replaced in most countries by displays of horsemanship, called carousels.

1600s The end of an era As warfare becomes the job of full-time soldiers and mercenaries, the era of chivalrous knights comes to an end.

Martin Luther preaching for a reformed Church in Germany

Find out **more**

There are many ways you can find out more about knights. Some of the best museums and castles are listed on the opposite page. Your local library and bookstore will also have plenty of books for you to read about knights, and there are often programs and movies on television and video for you to watch at home. Above all, check out the internet—some of the best websites to visit are listed below—and you too will soon become a dedicated knight-watcher.

Design a coat-of-arms

You can design your own or your family's coat-of-arms and use it to decorate your personal letters and belongings. The symbols you choose should be something special to you or have some connection to your name or to the place where you live.

The Great Hall, Warwick Castle

Narrow slit in helmet to see through

15th-century German Gothic-style armor

See a knight's armor

You can see knights' armor in many places throughout the UK and Europe. One of the best collections is in the Royal Armories in Leeds, Yorkshire.

Return to medieval times

You can visit a medieval castle and see how knights lived and fought in dramatic reconstructions of medieval life. In Warwick Castle, for example, you can see how a knight prepared for battle, and the magnificent Great Hall.

USEFUL WEBSITES

- Website listing Renaissance fairs across the country
  www.therenlist.com
- Website for the Tower of London
  www.hrp.org.uk/tower-of-london
- Take a virtual tour of the Philadelphia Museum of Art's vast arms and armor collection
  www.philamuseum.org
- For a virtual tour of the Metropolitan Museum's collection; search "arms and armor"
  www.metmuseum.org
- Samurai collection showcasing suits of armor, helmets, masks, weapons, and horse equipment
  www.samuraicollection.org/

Knights in frame

Many movies have been made about knights, such as *Ivanhoe* (1952), the story of a fictional disinherited knight. Based on the novel by Sir Walter Scott, several other film and TV versions of the story have been made. Sometimes, real-life knights have been portrayed in films, such as Rodrigo Díaz de Vivar of Spain in *El Cid*.

1952 poster showing Robert Taylor and Elizabeth Taylor

See fighting and jousting

Some historical reenactment groups put on displays of fighting or jousting today. Look in the useful websites box on the opposite page for more details. If you are lucky, you could even see a full-scale reenactment of a medieval tournament.

King Arthur

Sir Galahad is introduced to King Arthur

Modern-day jouster

Stories of King Arthur

You can read stories about knights in the tales of the legendary King Arthur and his knights of the round table. There is still dispute about who King Arthur was, or whether he actually existed at all, but some people now believe that he was a British chieftain or warrior who led the resistance to the Saxon invasion of England in the fifth or sixth century.

PLACES TO VISIT

THE METROPOLITAN MUSEUM OF ART, NEW YORK

Comprising over 14,000 objects, many from Europe and Asia, the Arms and Armor collection focuses on works that show outstanding design and decoration. It is one of the most comprehensive and encyclopedic collections of its kind.

THE PHILADELPHIA MUSEUM OF ART, ARMOR AND ARMS

Comprehensive and awe-inspiring collection of weaponry, suits of armor for both man and horse, and coats of arms, all crafted to the highest quality.

WARWICK CASTLE

A medieval castle that is also one of the finest stately homes in England. The main sights include:

- 14th-century ramparts and towers
- The armory, which features a massive 14th-century, two-hand sword

THE TOWER OF LONDON

This is the medieval fortress on the Thames River. Among the attractions here are:

- The White Tower, commissioned by William the Conqueror in 1078
- The Crown Jewels, which include the crowns, scepters, and orbs

OTHER MEDIEVAL CASTLES TO VISIT: LEEDS CASTLE, KENT

- A continuously inhabited castle ever since it was built in the 12th century

BODIAM CASTLE, EAST SUSSEX

- 14th-century castle with a tower at each corner surrounded by a moat

BAMBURGH CASTLE, NORTHUMBERLAND

- Overlooking the North Sea, the castle was inhabited by the Normans in the 11th century, and later became a military stronghold for the aristocracy

CAERPHILLY CASTLE, SOUTH WALES

- Fine example of a concentric castle surrounded by water and outer walls

EDINBURGH CASTLE, SCOTLAND

- Massive fortress, garrison, and one-time royal palace

CHÂTEAU DE SAUMUR, FRANCE

- A 14th-century castle that towers over the town of Saumur on the Loire River

Glossary

BALLISTA A weapon used in siege warfare, consisting of a giant crossbow that shot bolts.

BARBARIANS Uncivilized people. The word is often used to describe the tribes who invaded the Roman Empire in the 4th–5th centuries CE.

BATTLEMENT The top of a castle wall with gaps in it, through which archers could shoot at enemies.

BODKIN A long, thin arrowhead, shaped like a needle.

BOLT An arrow used for shooting from a crossbow or ballista.

BUTT A target set on a mound of earth, used by archers for shooting practice.

CATAPULT A device to launch missiles.

Bodkin

CHALICE A cup used to hold the wine in the Christian service of mass, or the Holy Communion.

CHIVALRY Originally meaning good horsemanship, chivalry came to refer to qualities expected of an ideal knight, such as courage, honor, courtesy, and, later, courtly manners toward women.

Embrasure in a castle wall

COAT-OF-ARMS A set of symbols used by a knight on his shield or surcoat to identify him in battle or at a tournament.

COAT-OF-PLATES A form of body armor consisting of many pieces of iron riveted to a cloth covering.

CROSSBOW A bow fixed across a wooden handle with a groove for a bolt. A cord was then released to shoot the bolt.

CRUSADES A series of military expeditions made by European knights during the Middle Ages, to capture the Holy Land and Spain from Muslim control.

DESTRIER A knight's warhorse.

DUBBING The ceremony at which a squire was made a knight.

EMBRASURE An alcove set in a castle wall with a small opening through which archers, crossbowmen, or gunners could shoot.

ETCHING Using acid to "eat" a design onto exposed parts of metal. Suits of armor were sometimes etched with patterns.

FEUDAL SYSTEM A social system used in Europe in the Middle Ages, whereby a local lord gave land to his vassals in return for their allegiance and service.

GARRISON A group of soldiers stationed in a castle or town to defend it.

GATEHOUSE The entrance to a castle, often protected with heavily fortified towers, a portcullis, drawbridge, and a ditch or moat outside.

GILDING Putting a thin covering of gold on an object to decorate it.

HERALDRY A system of using symbols on knights' shields, surcoats, banners, etc, so they could be easily identified in battle or in tournaments.

Gatehouse to Caerphilly Castle, Wales

HERETIC Someone whose religious views are unacceptable to the mainstream church.

INFANTRY Soldiers who fought on foot.

JOUST A combat between two mounted knights armed with lances.

KEEP A castle's stone tower, probably used as living quarters or for storage.

KNIGHT A warrior who fought on horseback. The term is normally used for the period c. 900–1600, when warriors fought with swords and lances.

KNIGHTS HOSPITALLER A military order of monks who also cared for the sick. They were also known as the Knights of St. John.

KNIGHTS TEMPLAR An order of monks who were also fighting knights. They fought against the Muslims and protected Christian pilgrims in the Holy Land.

LANCE A long weapon with a wooden shaft and a pointed metal head. Knights used lances when they were charging on horseback.

Joust at Tours in France, 1446

NGBOW A large bow used during e Middle Ages. It was usually made yew wood and could shoot arrows to 984 ft (300 m).

GS Two small cross-pieces on a spear sword that stopped the weapon ing pushed too far into an opponent's dy and getting stuck.

ACE A heavy weapon, consisting of a etal head and a wooden or metal haft.

ACHICOLATION A stone projection front of castle battlements through nich to drop stones or hot liquids n intruders.

AIL A form of armor made of many nall, linked iron rings. Mail could be ade up into garments, such as coats.

ERCENARY A hired soldier who ought simply for money.

OOR A Muslim from northwest Africa. he Moors also settled in Spain.

OTTE AND BAILEY An early style of astle. The motte was a mound with a ooden tower on top; the bailey was courtyard below the motte that ontained the domestic buildings.

ORMANS People who came from ormandy in northern France. The ormans were descended from

Armor of a Japanese samurai

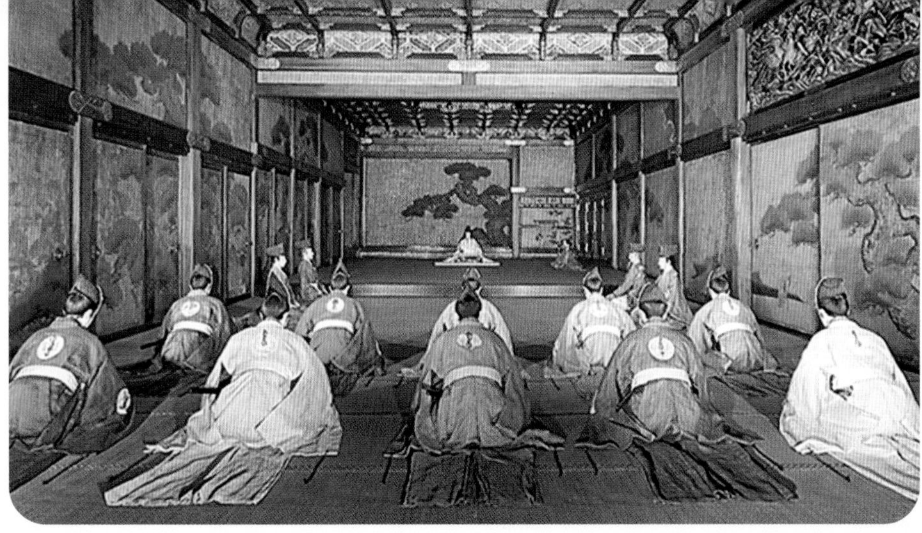
Reenactment of Japanese feudal lords paying their respects to the shogun

the Vikings who settled in the region during the 10th century. In 1066, the Normans conquered England under their leader, Duke William of Normandy.

PAGE A young boy serving in the household of a king, lord, or knight. He was in training to become a knight.

PALFREY A riding horse of good breeding for traveling or hunting.

PEASANT A farm laborer or other person who works for a lord.

PILGRIMAGE A journey to a sacred place for religious reasons. In the Middle Ages, some Christians went on pilgrimages to Jerusalem and to other sites in the Holy Land.

PLATE ARMOR Body armor made of metal or hardened leather, whalebone, or horn pieces, as opposed to mail.

POMMEL A round knob on the end of a sword handle, which helped balance the weight of the blade.

PORTCULLIS A metal gate, or an iron-clad wooden gate, which could be lowered in front of the entrance to a castle to stop attackers getting in.

RANSOM A sum of money demanded for the release of a prisoner captured or defeated in battle. The captors demanded the ransom from the prisoner's family.

SAMURAI A Japanese warrior.

SARACEN A name used at the time of the crusades for all Muslims and Arabs.

SCALING LADDER A long ladder used by attacking soldiers to try to climb over the wall of a castle.

SCONCE A candlestick for hanging on a wall.

SERF A laborer who was not allowed to leave the land on which he worked.

SHOGUN A Japanese military leader.

SHRINE A holy site, such as a saint's tomb.

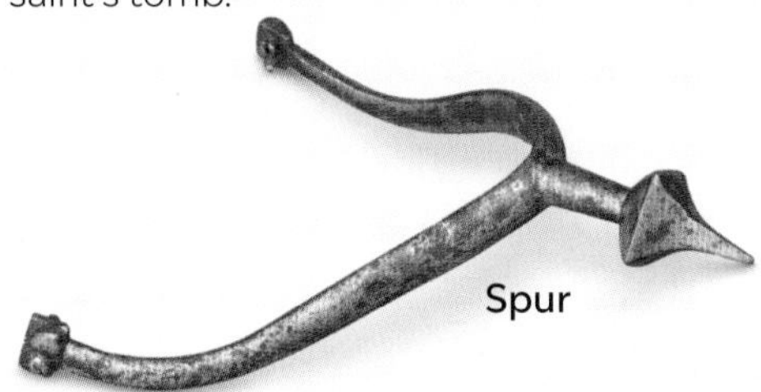
Spur

SPUR A spiked device that a knight fitted to his heels to urge his horse forward.

SQUIRE A young man who served a knight, often in training to become one.

STIRRUPS Two loops suspended from a horse's saddle to support the rider's feet.

SURCOAT A loose coat or robe worn over armor. It was sometimes decorated with the knight's coat-of-arms.

TILT A barrier used in jousting to separate the knights and avoid collisions.

TOURNAMENT A pageant that included mock battles, jousting, and foot combat, in which knights practiced their fighting.

TREBUCHET A weapon used in sieges to throw large missiles at a castle.

TROUBADOURS Medieval French poets who composed and sang poems on the theme of courtly love.

VISOR The movable part of a helmet that covered the face.

Index

A

Adams, Shane 44
Albigensian Crusade 55
archers 30-31, 33
armor 12-17, 28-29, 68
- foot combat 46, 47
- horses 15, 20-21
- jousting 45
- Muslim warriors 55
- professional soldiers 60-61
- samurai 58, 59

arms 18-19
arranged marriages 38, 39
arrows/arrowheads 30, 31
Arthur, King 41, 67, 69
axes 7, 19, 46

B

backplates 10, 28
badges of office 48
baileys 22
bailiffs 37
ballistas 27, 67
banners 15, 42, 49
Bannockburn, Battle of 30, 67
barbarians 6
barbutes 13
barriers 47
basinets 12, 46
battles 32-33
Bérenger, Raymond de 57
bevors 29
bits 21
boar hunts 51
board games 36
Bodiam Castle (UK) 24-25
breast plates 10, 28
burgonets 14, 61
butts 31

C

caltrops 32
Cambrai, Battle of 67
cannons 61, 67
Canterbury Tales, The (Chaucer) 53
Capwell, Dr. Tobias 13
Carlisle Roll 48
carousels 42
caskets 37
castles 22-23, 63, 64, 65, 66, 68, 69
- at war 24-25, 38
- life in 34-35

catapults 27, 67
Cathars 55
cavalry 6, 30, 32, 33, 60
chaffrons 21
chalices 52
chamber pots 35
champions, royal 41
Charlemagne 6, 7, 66
Charles III 63
Chaucer, Geoffrey 11, 53
chess 34, 36
Children's Crusade 64
chivalry 32, 40-41, 65, 66
church, the 9, 42, 52-55
club tourneys 43
coats-of-arms 48, 49, 62, 68
concentric castles 22
coursers 20
courtly manners/love 40, 67
Courtrai, Battle of 33
crossbows 26, 27, 31, 50-51
crosses, processional 53, 57
Crusades, the 54-55, 64, 65, 66, 67
cuirasses 10, 28, 58, 59
cuirassiers 60
cuisses 17, 28

D

daggers 18, 19, 29
de la Haye, Nicola 38
deer hunting 50
destriers 20, 21
ditches 22, 24
dogs, hunting 51
doublets, arming 28
dubbing 11
Dymoke, Sir Edward 41

EFG

Eleanor of Aquitaine 39
Elizabeth I 41
Elizabeth II 63
embrasures 25
face guards 14, 58, 59
falconry 50, 51
feudal system 6, 8, 60
films 62, 69
firearms 60, 61
fireplaces 34
flanking towers 25
foot combat 46-47, 58, 67
gatehouses 22, 24
gauntlets 12-13, 16, 29, 43
Grand Masters 57
greaves 28
Guinevere 41
gun batteries 61

H

halberds 61
Halder, Jacob 15
hand basins (gemellions) 35
hand gunners 60
Hangaku Gozen 59
Hastings, Battle of 8-9, 30, 66
hedge formation 30
helmets 7, 12, 13, 14, 16, 29
- foot combat 46, 61
- Japanese 58, 59
- jousting 44
- tournaments 42, 43

heraldry 48-49, 66
heralds 62
Holy Land 53, 54-55, 56, 57, 65
Holy Water 52
horns 9, 51, 52-53
horses 15, 20-21, 67
Hundred Years' War 67
hunting 39, 50-51
Hussites 30

IJK

infantry 60, 61
investiture ceremonies 63
Japanese knights 58-59, 67
Jerusalem 53, 54, 55, 64, 66
jewels 39
jousting 11, 20, 21, 42, 44-45, 46, 69
Kanne, Dr. Katherine 21
keeps 22, 23
kings, warrior 32
knighthoods, honorary 62, 63
Knights Hospitallers 56, 57
Knights of St. John 56, 57
Knights Templar 56, 57, 64, 66
knives, serving 35
Krak des Chevaliers (Syria) 64

L

ladies 38-39
ladies-in-waiting 38
Lancelot, Sir 41
lances 18, 19, 33, 44, 45, 60
leg guards 28
longbows 30, 31
lords 36-37
Louis XII of France 15
lures 50

M

maces 18
Magna Carta 36
mail 7, 12, 13, 28
Mamluks 55
manor lords and ladies 36-38
medicine 56, 57
mercenaries 36, 67
missionaries 53
moats 24
Molay, Jacques de 57
monks 52, 56
Moors 54
mottes 22
museums 68, 69
music and dance 34
Muslims 54-55, 56, 57
muzzles 21

NOP

nobles 7, 10, 11, 36-39
Normans 8-9, 66
Odo of Bayeux 9
Order of the Garter 63
orders of knighthood 65
pages 10
pauldrons 17
peasants 36, 37
pels 11
People's Crusade 54
peregrine falcons 50
Peter the Hermit 54
pikemen 60
pikes 30
pilgrimages 52-53, 64
plate armor 12, 13, 14, 28-29, 45, 60, 61, 67
poleaxes 46, 47
poleyns 17, 28, 47
professional armies 60-61, 62, 67
Protestantism 52

R

reading 38, 39
reenactments, battle 62-63
Reformation, the 67
relics 53
religious faith 52-53, 54-55
Rhodes missal 56-57
Richard I the Lionheart 39, 54, 64, 65, 67
Rochester Castle (UK) 23
Rollo 8
Roman Catholicism 52, 55, 57, 67
Roman Empire 6
romances, medieval 40, 41, 67
Romanesque architecture 9
rounceys 20

S

sabatons 28
saddles 39
saints 52, 53
Saladin 55
samurai 58-59
scabbards 29
scaling ladders 25, 26
seals 32, 36, 52, 57
shields 8, 13, 44
- heraldry 48-49

ships 8, 49, 54
shoguns 58, 67
siege warfare 25, 26-27, 64, 66-67
skirts, mail 28
Slavs 54
slingers 30
Smithsonian Castle (USA) 63
Spanish crusaders 54
spears 6, 51
spoils of war 33
spurs 20, 29
squires 10, 11, 66
St. Ubaldesca 56
stirrups 7, 20
suits of armor 14-15, 47, 59, 60, 61, 67
sumpters 20
surrender 27
swords 7, 9, 18-19, 29, 49, 67
- samurai 58-59
- two-handed 18, 60

T

tabards 62
Talhoffer, Hans 18
Teutonic Knights 56, 57, 67
tournaments 42-43, 62, 65, 66
training 10, 31
trebuchets 26, 27, 64, 66
trial by battle 46
Tristan and Iseult 41
troubadours 40, 67
true-love knots 40
Turks 54

UVW

Urban II, Pope 54
vambraces 17, 29
vamplates 43
Vikings 10, 22, 66
visors 42
wall sconces 34
walls, defensive 22, 23
weapons see arms
Welsh archers 31
wheel-lock pistols 61
William I the Conqueror 8, 65
wolf hunts 50
women 38-39

Acknowledgments

The publisher would like to thank the following for their help with making the book:
The Wallace Collection, the Royal Armouries, the British Museum, and the Museum of the Order of St John, for provision of objects for photography; English Heritage, the National Trust, and Cadw (Welsh Historical Monuments), for permission to photograph at Rochester, Bodiam, & Caerphilly castles; David Edge for information on items in the Wallace Collection; Paul Cannings, Jonathan Waller, John Waller, Bob Dow, Ray Monery, & Julia Harris for acting as models; Anita Burger for make-up; Joanna Cameron for illustrations (pages 22-23); Angels & Burmans for costumes; Bipasha Roy for editorial assistance; Abhimanyu Adhikary for design assistance; Vagisha Pushp for picture research assistance; Hazel Beynon for proofreading; and Helen Peters for the index.

For a previous edition, the publisher would also like to thank:
the author for assisting with revisions; Claire Bowers, David Ekholm-JAlbum, Sunita Gahir, Joanne Little, Nigel Ritchie, Susan St Louis, Carey Scott, & Bulent Yusuf for the clipart; David Ball, Neville Graham, Rose Horridge, Joanne Little, & Sue Nicholson for the wallchart; BCP, Marianne Petrou, & Owen Peyton Jones for checking the digitized files.

The publisher would like to thank the following for their kind permission to reproduce their images:
(Key: a-above; b-below/bottom; c-center; f-far; l-left; r-right; t-top)

Alamy Stock Photo: Abbus Archive Images 55tl, Album 49bc, 54cl, Allstar Picture Library Ltd 69tl, Associated Press / Uncredited 63cr, Andrew Barker 36tr, CPA Media Pte Ltd / Pictures From History 55cb, 57bc, Digital-Fotofusion Gallery 38br, Florilegius 49clb, GRANGER - Historical Picture Archive 29c, 30bl, 50tr, Shim Harno 13br, Historic Images 18cra, 53clb, IanDagnall Computing 7br, 39tl, Interfoto / Fine Arts 8-9b, Interfoto / History 19bc, Japan Art Collection (JAC) 58cr, 59bc, Jimlop collection 17cr, North Wind Picture Archives 36cl, Penta Springs Limited / Artokoloro 14br, Photo 12 54-55b, The Picture Art Collection 40br, Pictures Now 31bl, The Print Collector / Heritage Images 52c, Prisma Archivo 34tl, Prisma by Dukas Presseagentur GmbH / TPX 9cl, Reading Room 2020 27cla, 27ca, Science History Images / Photo Researchers 6ca, stocker123 24-25b, Wojciech Stróyk 13tr, The History Collection 32-33t, 57tc, Colin Waters 37tc, World History Archive 11tr. **Ancient Art & Architecture Collection:** 58cl, 58c, 58tr, 59bl, 65b. **Board of the Trustees of the Armouries:** 70tl. **Bridgeman Images:** 40-41t, 43t, 55tr, 53b, Biblioteca Estense, Modena: 10b, Bibliotheque de L'Arsenal, Paris: 64br, British Library: 19tc, 20tr, 20c, 39c, 49tr, 54tl, Bibliotheque Municipal de Lyon: 55cl, Bibliotheque Nationale, Paris: 15tr, 22cr, 25tl, 41cr, 42bl, Corpus Christi College, Cambridge: 13tl, Musee Conde, Chantilly: 50bc, 51bl, 65t, Vatican Library, Rome: 50br, Victoria & Albert Museum: 37cl, Wrangham Collection: 59c, From the British Library archive 11crb, 45bl, © Germanisches National Museum 7crb, © Lambeth Palace Library 48c, © Photo Josse 33bl, Photo © CSG CIC Glasgow Museums Collection 14l, Photo © Leonard de Selva 56bl, Photo: Philadelphia Museum of Art / Gift of Elizabeth Malcolm Bowman in memory of Wendell Phillips Bowman, 1930 62tl, Luisa Ricciarini 6-7b, 63cla. **© The Trustees of the British Museum. All rights reserved:** 2cl, 39tr, 53r. **Burgerbibliothek, Bern:** 25rc. **Dorling Kindersley:** Photo from Children just Like Me by Barnabus & Anabel Kindersley, published by DK: 71bl, Geoff Dann / Wallace Collection, London 18-19b. **Dreamstime.com:** Patrick Guenette 21c, Jiawangkun 63tc, Anne Kitzman 44br, Mestiv5 62-63b. **Getty Images:** Hulton Archive 9cr, Roger Viollet / Pierre Barbier 57tr. **Getty Images / iStock:** DigitalVision Vectors / whitemay 11bl, wynnter 46br. **Katherine Kanne:** Helene Benkert 21cra. **Mary Evans Picture Library:** 69bl. **The Metropolitan Museum of Art:** Gift of Stephen V. Grancsay, 1942 20bl, 71cr. **Robert Harding Picture Library:** 8cl, 12rc, 22bl, 34br, 34bl, British Library: 11c, 34c. **© Royal Armouries:** 47r. **Heritage Images:** British Library 46bl. **Bildarchiv Foto Marburg:** 48br. **Shutterstock.com:** Harper Collins Publishers 27clb, 48cr, Alfredo Dagli Orti 27cra, 33crb, Eileen Tweed 41bl, 60tr, Eileen Tweedy 59cla, Federico Zovadelli 55br. **Warwick Castle:** 68cb.

WHAT WILL YOU EYEWITNESS NEXT?

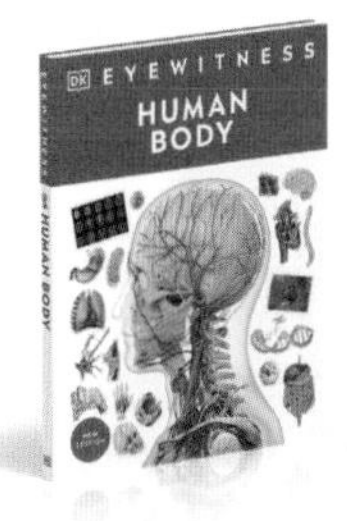

Also available:

Eyewitness Amphibian
Eyewitness Ancient China
Eyewitness Ancient Civilizations
Eyewitness Arms and Armor
Eyewitness Astronomy
Eyewitness Aztec, Inca & Maya
Eyewitness Baseball
Eyewitness Bible Lands
Eyewitness Car

Eyewitness Castle
Eyewitness Chemistry
Eyewitness Dance
Eyewitness Earth
Eyewitness Eagle and Birds of Prey
Eyewitness Electricity
Eyewitness Endangered Animals
Eyewitness Forensic Science
Eyewitness Gandhi
Eyewitness Great Scientists

Eyewitness Islam
Eyewitness Judaism
Eyewitness Jungle
Eyewitness Medieval Life
Eyewitness Mesopotamia
Eyewitness Money
Eyewitness Mummy
Eyewitness Mythology
Eyewitness North American Indian
Eyewitness Pirate

Eyewitness Plant
Eyewitness Prehistoric Life
Eyewitness Presidents
Eyewitness Robot
Eyewitness Science
Eyewitness Shakespeare
Eyewitness Skeleton
Eyewitness Soldier
Eyewitness Space Exploration
Eyewitness Vietnam War